PAUL GARRETT

DEAN OF AMERICAN WINEMAKERS

Emerson Klees

Emerson Klees

Cameo Press Imprint

Friends of the Finger Lakes Publishing, Rochester, New York

Copyright © 2010 by Emerson C. Klees

All rights reserved. This book, or parts thereof, may not be reproduced in any form without permission.

Friends of the Finger Lakes Publishing
P. O. Box 18131
Rochester, New York 14618

Library of Congress Control Number 2010933706

ISBN 978-1-891046-10-0

Printed in the United States of America
9 8 7 6 5 4 3 2 1

This book is dedicated to my classmate for sixteen years and good friend for a lifetime, Esther Donovan Jackson. Esther was my surrogate sister—the sister that I never had. She could always be counted on for sisterly advice. When I became a vineyardist and amateur winemaker, she volunteered to pick grapes in my small vineyard every autumn. Esther, who passed away in February 2009, is missed by all who knew her.

Other Books by Emerson Klees

The Human Values Series

Role Models of Human Values

One Plus One Equals Three—Pairing Man / Woman Strengths:
   Role Models of Teamwork (1998)
Entrepreneurs in History—Success vs. Failure:
   Entrepreneurial Role Models (1999)
Staying With It: Role Models of Perseverance (1999)
The Drive to Succeed: Role Models of Motivation (2002)
The Will to Stay With It: Role Models of Determination (2002)

The Moral Navigator

Inspiring Legends and Tales With a Moral I: Stories From
   Around the World (2007)
Inspiring Legends and Tales With a Moral II: Stories From
   Around the World (2007)
Inspiring Legends and Tales With a Moral III: Stories From
   Around the World (2007)

Books about New York State and the Finger Lakes Region

People of the Finger Lakes Region (1995)
Legends and Stories of the Finger Lakes Region (1995)
The Erie Canal in the Finger Lakes Region (1996)
Underground Railroad Tales With Routes Through the
   Finger Lakes Region (1997)
More Legends and Stories of the Finger Lakes Region (1997)
The Women's Rights Movement and the Finger Lakes Region (1998)
Persons, Places, and Things In the Finger Lakes Region (2000)
The Crucible of Ferment: New York's Psychic Highway (2001)
The Iroquois Confederacy: History and Legends (2003)
Rochester Lives (2004)
Wineries of the Finger Lakes Region (2008)
Person, Places, and Things Of the Finger Lakes Region (2009)

PREFACE

"Paul Garrett was evidently born to be a salesman, and since wine was given to him to sell, sell it he did. His ability to sell was so far in excess of the winery's ability to produce that he eventually left it to operate on his own as Garrett & Company, founded in 1900. At first he contracted to sell New York State wines as well as those of North Carolina, but he soon determined to concentrate his efforts on the wine from the Scuppernong grape of his native state. He was inspired to call his most popular Scuppernong wine Virginia Dare, after the first child born to English settlers in this country, on the island [Roanoke] where the Scuppernong vine itself was thought to have originated.

"So popular did Virginia Dare become, in fact, that its sales outstripped the supply of Scuppernong grapes. Garrett had constantly to exhort the farmers of North Carolina to plant more to feed his presses, and when his efforts fell short of his needs he had to resort to changing the formula: Virginia Dare may have begun as a pure Scuppernong wine, but as its popularity grew so did the volume of bulk California wine that Garrett was forced to add to it. In the end, it had only enough Scuppernong juice in it to 'tincture the flavor.'"

Thomas Pinney, *A History of Wine in America from
the Beginnings to Prohibition*

Captain Paul Garrett, dean of American winemakers in the first two decades of the twentieth century, became a multimillionaire making and selling wine. The title of "captain" was not of military origin but was what his employees called him when they did not call him "boss." He was born in North Carolina in 1863 and by the age of 14 was working for Medoc Vineyard, North Carolina's first commercial winery, owned by his father, country doctor Francis Garrett, and his uncle, Charles Garrett, who ran the winery.

Garrett promoted wine made from the southern Scuppernong grape. He chose for his wine the name Virginia Dare—the first child born of English parents in America—because it symbolized wholesomeness and purity and was the first popular American commercial wine.

Garrett established his first winery, Garrett & Company, in North Carolina in 1900, and by 1903, he owned five wineries in that state. He expanded into other states, and by 1913, he owned vineyards and facilities in Canandaigua, Hammondsport, and Penn Yan in New York State, as well as Mission Vineyard and Winery in Cucamonga, California. In 1919, he owned 17 plants processing grape juice or wine with a capacity of 10 million gallons in the States of California, Missouri, New York, North Carolina, Ohio, and Virginia.

With the advent of Prohibition, Garrett could have retired as a multimillionaire, but he held on to his wine empire, not believing that Prohibition would last. He lost money on de-alcoholized wine, a cola-flavored grape drink, flavoring extracts, and grape concentrates. However, when Prohibition was repealed in 1933, he was the only vintner capable of marketing wine in every Wet state. Also, he was the first winery executive to promote wine made from blending New York State and California juices.

Garrett's theme was "American wine for Americans." He was in New York City promoting that idea when he contracted pneumonia following surgery and died on March 18, 1940, at the age of 76. He truly was a captain in his industry.

TABLE OF CONTENTS

LIST OF PHOTOGRAPHS, ILLUSTRATIONS, AND MAPS

Front cover: Paul Garrett, Virginia Dare, and Muscadine Grapes
Back Cover: Bluff Point, Keuka Lake
Inside the book: *Page No.*

Paul Sprague, Director, Greyton H. Taylor Wine Museum, provided valuable suggestions and source material about Paul Garrett.

Cover design by Dunn and Rice Design, Inc., Rochester, New York

Maps by ActionMaps, Rochester, New York

The vector art images used herein were obtained from IMSI's MasterClips Collection, 1895 Francisco Blvd. East, San Rafael, California 94901-5506, USA.

PROLOGUE

The History of Winemaking in the Eastern United States

"The Eastern United States, with its largely untapped potential for wine production, is a new frontier for American wine much as the West once was for American pioneers. Establishing a vineyard and winery east of the Rockies has many parallels with homesteading in the Old West: developing a modus operandi in a new environment, aiming to transform dreams into realities. . . .

"An advantage of winegrowing in the East is that the climate produces fresh-tasting wines, with higher acidity and lower alcoholic content than most from California, the largest wine-producing state. . . . If variety is the spice of life, the most flavorful wine region of all lies east of the Rockies. The East's many climates and cornucopia of grape varieties provide an exciting challenge for wine adventurers—whether the adventure is producing one's own wine or enjoying new experiences in wine tasting."

Lucie T. Morton, *Winegrowing in Eastern America:*
An Illustrated Guide to Viticulture East of the Rockies

Around 1000 AD, Leif, the Lucky, Ericsson, son of Eric the Red, discovered a land where there was "no lack of grapes or vines." It is thought that he landed in either what is now Rhode Island or Massachusetts. In 1694, Governor William Penn established a vineyard on the east bank of the Schuylkill River in Philadelphia in which he attempted to grow *Vitis vinifera* (European) grapes. Vine pests and diseases caused his experiment to fail. Pollen from this vineyard was carried to a wild native *Vitis labrusca* vine to create the red Alexander grape.

In 1740, John Alexander, gardener of Lieutenant Governor John Penn, found a grapevine growing along the Schuylkill River and transplanted it to Penn's garden. The Alexander grape was more winter hardy and disease resistant than the *Vitis vinifera* varieties planted earlier. In 1793, Pierre Legaux established the Pennsylvania Wine Company at his Spring Mill vineyard and became the first commercial vineyardist in the United States. His principal grape was the Alexander.

Thomas Jefferson tried unsuccessfully for many years to establish a wine industry in Virginia. His interest in wine increased during his years as U.S. Minister to France. He gave 2,000 acres adjacent to Monticello to Philip Mazzei, a vineyardist from Italy.

In 1773, Mazzei brought 10,000 *Vitis vinifera* vine cuttings from Tuscany along with trained vineyardists to plant and care for them. However, the Revolutionary War shifted Jefferson's priority away from his vineyard project.

In 1809, Jefferson wrote to grape-growing pioneer John Adlum:

> Sir:
> While I lived in Washington, a member of Congress from your state presented me with . . . wine made by you; a dark red wine made from a wild or native grape. This was a very fine wine, and so exactly resembling the red Burgundy of Chambertin that on fair comparison with that, of which I had very good on the same table imported by myself from the place where made, the company could not distinguish one from the other. I think that it would be well to push the culture of that grape without losing our time and efforts in search of foreign vines, which it will take centuries to adapt to our soil and climate.

Adlum replied to Jefferson that the wine similar to Chambertin was made from Alexander grapes, a *Vitis vinifera-Vitis labrusca* hybrid. Alexander was the first variety to move out of the hedgerows and onto trellises in cultivated vineyards in the U.S. Jefferson's advice was taken. The first vineyards in Ohio, Pennsylvania, and Indiana were planted with Alexander grapevines during the early 1800s. In 1818, the first commercial vineyards for wine grapes were planted by Thomas Eichelberger in York, Pennsylvania, near the Susquehanna River.

During the next 50 years, the Alexander grape was overshadowed by improved varieties such as Isabella, introduced by William Prince of Flushing, New York, in 1816; Catawba by John Adlum of Washington, D.C., in 1823; Concord by Ephram Bull of Concord, Massachusetts, in 1852; and Elvira by Jacob Rommel of Missouri in 1870.

In 1825, Nicholas Longworth, a Cincinnati lawyer, purchased Catawba vines from John Adlum and planted vineyards along the Ohio River. Longworth's sparkling Catawba was the first sparkling wine made in the United States. Ohio became the leading wine-producing state during the 1850s. Catawba was the favorite wine grape except in the South, where Scuppernong was preferred.

By the 1860s, Longworth's Catawba vineyards along the Ohio River were struggling. Diseases that had destroyed the early *Vitis vinifera* vineyards were attacking Catawba vines planted in the humid climate of southern Ohio. Powdery mildew, which thrives in hot, dry conditions; downy mildew that favors cool, moist climates; and black rot, which prospers in warm, humid conditions, decimated Catawba plantings as it had *Vitis vinifera* vineyards earlier.

Sulfur was effective against powdery mildew but was ineffective against downy mildew and black rot. Bordeaux mixture, a combination of copper sulfate, lime, and water was developed to control downy mildew and black rot in 1885—too late to save the vineyards in southern Ohio. Ohio's grape-growing region shifted to the cooler climate of northern Ohio along Lake Erie. In the 1860s, Missouri became the leading grower of wine grapes.

In the mid-1800s, a viticultural disaster occurred. Native vine cuttings had been sent from America to Europe for experimentation and hybridization with *Vitis vinifera* varieties. The aphid Phylloxera had accompanied the vine cuttings to Europe. Vines in old, established vineyards began to die for unknown reasons. The French government funded research to save the country's six million acres of vineyards.

Research showed that if vineyardists grafted *Vitis vinifera* vines onto disease-resistant rootstock, European varieties could survive against the Phylloxera. Grafting helped the French wine industry survive but increased the cost of making wine.

Although the industry recovered, acreage of wine grapes decreased from six million acres to three million acres in France. While grafting was effective against Phylloxera, it did not provide protection against vine diseases such as powdery mildew, downy mildew, and black rot.

Hermann Jaeger of Missouri and T. V. Munson of Texas sent cuttings to France to help the Europeans develop Phylloxera-resistant rootstocks and *Vitis vinifera-Vitis labrusca* hybrids. In 1888, Jaeger and Munson were awarded the French Legion of Honor in appreciation of their assistance during the Phylloxera crisis. Munson was the author of *Foundations of American Grape Culture*.

Grape growing in New York State developed in three regions: the Hudson River Valley, the Finger Lakes Region, and the Chautauqua Region along Lake Erie. In 1829 in the rectory garden of St. James Episcopal Church in Hammondsport, Reverend William Bostwick planted the first grapevines in the Finger Lakes Region, Catawba and Isabella vines from the Hudson River Valley.

In 1839, Blooming Grove Winery was established by Jean Jacques in Washingtonville to make altar wines. This Hudson River Valley winery, later called Brotherhood Winery, is the oldest active winery in the United States.

The Chautauqua Region became the largest grape-growing region in the state by focusing on growing *Vitis labrusca* varieties, such as Concord, for grape juice. The area along Lake Erie became the principal supplier of grapes to Welch's.

Publisher Horace Greeley called the Concord variety "the grape for the millions." In 1866, Concord was awarded the Greeley Prize as the best all-around grape variety. It is an adaptable and disease-resistant grape that is productive and easy to grow. However, its foxy or grapey taste prevented it from becoming an acceptable wine grape. Better wine could be made from Cynthiana and Norton varieties, but they were not as easy to grow or as hardy as Concord.

Late in the nineteenth century, the temperance movement gained momentum. In the 1870s, prohibitionist dentist Dr. Thomas Welch's grape juice ("unfermented wine") gained popularity. Grape growers were willing to plant additional acres of Concord instead of more-difficult-to-grow wine grapes. The most popular wine in the years prior to the beginning of Prohibition in 1919 was Garrett & Company's Virginia Dare, a blend of Scuppernong, Concord, and California *Vitis vinifera*. The taste of Scuppernong dominated, despite the strong taste of Concord.

The temperance movement gained momentum slowly, beginning with the 1816 law in Indiana banning the sale of alcoholic beverages on Sunday. During the 1840s, many towns and counties in the East and Midwest went Dry. Entire states began to go Dry, beginning with Kansas in 1880 and Iowa in 1882. On January 16, 1919, the Eighteenth Amendment (the Prohibition Amendment) to the Constitution was ratified.

Many wineries went out of business. Some tried to stay profitable by producing medicinal and sacramental wines for a very small market. On December 5, 1933, the Twenty-first Amendment to the Constitution was ratified, repealing Prohibition.

Three individuals, in addition to Paul Garrett, contributed heavily to helping the U.S. wine industry recover from Prohibition: Frank Schoonmaker of New York City, Philip Wagner of Maryland, and Leon Adams of California. Garrett died in 1940. Many changes in the wine industry occurred in the several decades after his death.

Schoonmaker was a wine importer and author of the *Complete Wine Book (1934), American Wines (1941),* and *The Encyclopedia of Wine* (1973). Although he was an importer of European wines, he was optimistic about grape growing and winemaking in the United States. By emphasizing the selection of the appropriate grape varieties for each growing region, he correctly identified one of the early shortcomings of growing wine grapes in America. He advocated varietal labeling instead of relying exclusively on blends.

Philip Wagner, editor of the Baltimore *Sun*, went beyond wine appreciation; he became a grape grower, winemaker, and author of *American Wines and How To Make Them* (1933), *A Wine-Growers Guide* (1973), and *Grapes Into Wine: The Art of Winemaking in*

America (1976). Wagner realized that growing *Vitis vinifera* grapes in his Maryland vineyard would be difficult.

Wagner read French grape-growing literature and discovered hybrids of American and European grape varieties developed in France. He visited France in 1936-37 and found that these hybrids were being used principally as wine grapes, and that some of them had been sent to vineyardists in the U.S.

In 1942, Wagner established a commercial nursery to provide French-American hybrid vines to U.S. grape growers. In 1945, Wagner established a bonded winery, Boordy Vineyards, in Penn Yan, New York, to produce wine from hybrid grapes. Earlier, the facility had been a Garrett & Company winery.

Leon Adams, journalist, wine historian, and wine pioneer, advocated drinking wine in moderation. In 1931, he founded the California Grape Growers League that preceded the establishment of the Wine Institute in 1934 and the Wine Advisory Board in 1938. Board money financed grape research at universities, establishment of wine quality standards, and lobbyists to work with state governments, the federal government, and international wine organizations.

In 1942, Adams wrote *The Wine Study Course*, followed by *The Common Sense Book of Wine* in 1958 and *The Common Sense Book of Drinking* in 1960. In 1973, he wrote his classic book, *The Wines of America*. Adams traveled around the country as well as Canada and Mexico for 20 years visiting wineries to inquire about their new developments in grape growing and winemaking, gathering material for his book.

Adams urged grape growers to work with their state legislators and departments of agriculture to allow wineries at their vineyards. In 1968, Pennsylvania was the first state to pass a "limited winery" law. Limited wineries became known as "farm wineries," and for the first time in the U.S., a vineyardist did not have to go through the formal, expensive process of becoming a bonded winery to produce and sell wine. Leon Adams became known as the "father of farm wineries."

The most significant change in the wine industry in the eastern U.S. began in the late 1950s and early 1960s with the introduction of *Vitis vinifera* grape varieties, such as Chardonnay, Riesling, Cabernet Sauvignon, and Pinot Noir by Dr. Konstantin Frank in the

Finger Lakes Region. He had grown *Vitis vinifera* varieties in Ukraine along the Dneiper River, where the temperature went to 40 below zero.

Dr. Frank pointed out that *Vitis Vinifera* vines did not die from the cold, but from disease, such as mildew and fungus, as well as from vine pests; furthermore, modern technology controlled these problems. The combination of small boutique wineries and wine made from Vinifera grapes changed eastern U.S. winemaking forever.

Paul Garrett (1863-1940)

CHAPTER 1

The Garrett Family and Early Life

"During the vintage season, at which time we not only used our own grapes but bought grapes from all neighboring vineyards over an area of 40 to 50 miles, I was at my desk every morning between 5:50 a.m. and 6:00 a.m. . . . With fall approaching, we generally loaded out every morning from two to five wagons, and it was my business to personally see that the load was distributed . . . I generally personally placed the load on the wagons, learning to handle a 500-pound barrel of wine as easily as the average boy of my age [mid-teens] would handle a keg of nails or a barrel of flour.

"I took a great deal of pride in using my mind to use my strength intelligently, the rule having been inculcated upon me by my uncle that what was worth doing at all was worth doing promptly and to the very best of an intelligent ability. As the grapes ripened and we got in labor, frequently numbering 300 men, women, and children . . . I put in 18 hours a day in keeping up my bookkeeping, supervising the shipping, supervising and actually working in the wine-making."

Paul Garrett, *Reminiscences*

The family to which Paul Garrett belonged was thought to have been descended from a Jamestown colony settler listed on the boat roster as "John James Garrett, honest carpenter." A branch of his family settled in Pitt County, North Carolina.

Paul Garrett's maternal grandfather, Col. David Williams, served in the Mexican War and led his company in the Battle of Chepultepec. The Garrett family were agriculturalists and professional men. The generation preceding Garrett's generation consisted of six brothers, all successful in different careers, leaders in the financial, social, and political arenas in their communities.

Paul Garrett was born in Edgecombe County, North Carolina, on November 3, 1863, to Dr. Francis Marion Garrett, a Confederate Army surgeon, and Della Elizabeth Williams Garrett. Dr. Garrett graduated from the Pennsylvania Medical College in Philadelphia and interned at Bellevue Hospital in New York. At birth, Paul's twin brother, Phillip, was the sturdier child. Paul was affected with colic and was told later in life that his brother had a much better disposition. Unfortunately, Phillip died at the age of six months.

Paul's mother died when he was in his early teens. His father remarried, but Paul and his stepmother were not very close. He had several cousins with whom he was close. His cousin Margaret had been 14 when her mother died, and she had to assume the duties of head of the family. She was only a few months older than Paul, but she matured early due to her family responsibilities.

Paul considered Margaret the individual who had the most influence on him during the formative period of his character in his early teens. The affection between them was that of good friends. Margaret had an outgoing personality. She was the organizer of all the social activities for the teenage set, and Paul was her first lieutenant.

Paul was healthy as a young man; nevertheless, he vividly recalled suffering from a case of typhoid fever. His health started to improve and then took a turn for the worse. His temperature climbed to 105. He had something akin to an out-of-body experience.

Paul's visions seemed very real. He had passed away, and the casket was brought in and he was placed in it. He said that his "spirit" rode with the driver of the family wagon that carried the casket to the churchyard. He listened to the services being conducted—his own funeral services. Personally, he did not feel sad. Nevertheless, he recalled being distressed at seeing his friends and classmates crying as his casket was lowered into the grave. When he awoke, he did not feel relieved to have survived.

Paul's cousin Lucy was his chief nurse. She read to him often and was very helpful in scratching his head when it needed it. Slowly, his health improved, and he gained back the weight that he had lost. That was the only illness that he ever had. Later in life, when doctors told him to slow down or he might die from over-work, he ignored them. In his opinion, hard work was keeping him alive. After all, he had been given a second chance in life.

Paul was educated at the local school in Ringwood. He was a good student, but mathematics was not one of his strong subjects. His father tutored him in Latin. One of his teachers, Miss Jasper, appealed to Paul's ambition to excel in school. Miss Jasper was also a strong influence on another of her pupils, Walter H. Page, who became U.S. Ambassador to England during World War I. Page was also a noted figure in the literary world with Doubleday & Company and was a relative of one of Paul's friends.

Paul also attended Bingham Academy in Alamance County, North Carolina, when he was thirteen. His first three months at the school were the unhappiest of his young life. Although he per-formed well on the baseball field and adapted to the routine of mil-itary drill, the academy seemed to crush all of the free spirit out of him.

Paul had difficulty dealing with being placed in the freshman class, even though, academically, he was ready for the sophomore or junior class. He found out later that this was common practice in preparatory schools. He spent most of his time tutoring his class-mates.

Finally, Paul scheduled a meeting with the principal, Major Bingham, to tell him that he was going to drop out of school. Bingham told him that if he dropped out in mid-term, he would regret it for the rest of his life, because he would be viewed as a failure. He encouraged Paul to stay in school at least until the end of the term. He promised to move him to classes that were more challenging and kept that promise.

One incident that Paul remembered from his youth was a hang-ing party. The neighborhood was aroused by the disappearance of a highly regarded workman from the farm adjacent to the Garrett property. A thorough search turned up the body of the man, who had been killed on the adjoining farm. The shoes of the slain man were missing. When his shoes were discovered being worn by the son of a loyal Garrett employee, what had begun as a search party turned into an unruly mob.

A rope was thrown over the branch of a tree in the Garrett's front yard, and a noose placed around the young man's neck. The mob was going to hang him without a trial. Paul's father, accompanied only by a sturdily built cousin, held off the mob and took the accused man to the county jail. In the trial that followed, the young man was acquitted on a technicality and continued to work on the Garrett farm. Paul knew that his father was fearless, having seen examples of his father's willingness to stand up for what he thought was right on other occasions. Paul respected and looked up to his father as a role model.

In 1867, Garrett's father and uncle, Charles Garrett, purchased Medoc Vineyard, the first commercial winery in North Carolina, which had been established in 1835 by Sidney Weller in neighboring Halifax County at Brinckleyville. The vineyard had 8,000 Scuppernong vines, 2,000 Concord vines, and small numbers of other native varieties, such as Delaware and Iona. The annual production from one five-acre section that contained 400 Scuppernong vines ranged from 3,000 to 5,000 gallons.

Charles Garrett, who ran the winery, played an important role in Garrett's formative years. At the age of 17, he decided to participate in the California gold rush of 1849. He traveled to New York to obtain passage to California but missed the sailing of the ship. He went to work for a large clothing manufacturer, and, when the owner retired, he purchased the company with the aid of long-term loans. By the age of 30, Charles Garrett had amassed a fortune of two to three million dollars. Unfortunately, his health became impaired to the extent that he was advised to give up his demanding business life and retire to a farm.

When Paul dropped out of school in 1877 at the age of 14, he assisted his uncle Charles in running his winery. Paul moved in with this aunt Mary and uncle and learned all facets of the wine business. He worked long hours, five or six days a week over the next seven years, keeping the books, handling the correspondence,

filling orders, and making wine. He knew the theory of grape growing but realized that it was not one of his strengths. He considered
himself more of an agriculturalist than a farmer.

In 1883, Charles died, and the winery was taken over by his
son-in-law, Spooner Harrison. Charles had asked Harrison to
ensure that Paul Garrett, with seven years of experience at the winery, be kept on. Nevertheless, Harrison told Garrett to look for
another job. Garrett became a salesman on the road, working under
the direction of brothers Sy and June Wright, who were the principal marketing agents for C. W. Garrett & Company, parent of
Medoc Vineyard. Paul's experiences with the winery and his sales
training with the Wright brothers provided him with an excellent
background in the wine industry. This experience and his strong
work ethic were significant factors in his later success.

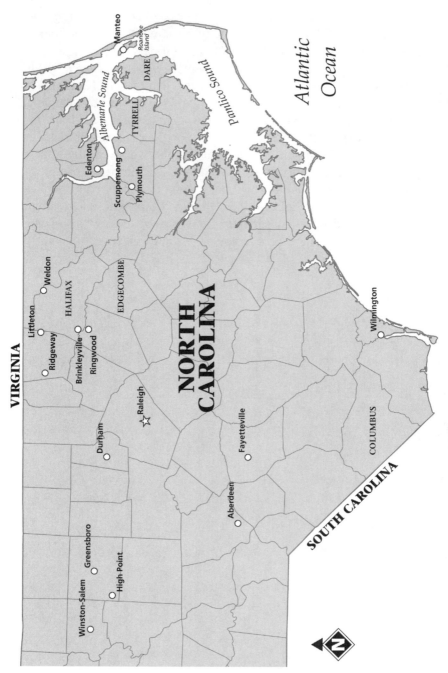

Map of North Carolina, east of the Piedmont Region

CHAPTER 2

Grape Growing / Winemaking in North Carolina

"The [Scuppernong] grape is a [variety] of the wild Muscadine grape (*Vitis rotundiflora*), native only to the Southern states . . . By 1840 North Carolina was ranked the number-one wine producer of the Union, a distinction then of small economic concern and one soon lost to Georgia and other states . . . Wine pressed from the Muscadines by commercial vintners occasionally won awards in Vienna and Paris, and in 1904, a bottle of sparkling Scuppernong made by a Carolina firm captured the prestigious blue ribbon for champagne with the Louisiana Purchase Exposition in St. Louis.

"The winner was Paul Garrett, who started his notable career as America's chief vintner in Halifax County, North Carolina, and eventually reaped a huge fortune from a veritable grape empire extending from coast to coast. Garrett made the Scuppernong the most popular wine of the United States in the years just prior to the advent of national Prohibition, under the name Virginia Dare."

Clarence Gohdes, *Scuppernong: North Carolina's Grape and Its Wines*

The Scuppernong grape variety first attracted the attention of wine-makers during the last half of the eighteenth century in the area of present-day Columbia, North Carolina. The variety was found growing prolifically in Tyrrell County, along the banks of a stream called the Scuppernong that flows into an arm of Albemarle Sound. At the head of the stream was a body of inland water called Scuppernong Lake. A nearby town was also called Scuppernong. The Scuppernong grape was named for a stream, which was named for a tree. "Ascopo" was the Algonquin Indian name for the sweet bay or bay laurel tree.

In addition to the Scuppernong area of Tyrrell County, the "Big White Grape" was also identified with Roanoke Island. So many vines were planted there by resident fishermen that the name Roanoke was widely associated with the popular Muscadine. According to legend, Sir Walter Raleigh obtained the original vines and had them planted for the use of the colony there. Many people believed that a vine in Manteo, North Carolina, was the mother of all Scuppernong. It was called the "Mother" vine.

Scuppernong was called the Big White Grape until census taker James Blount of the Town of Scuppernong took the census of Washington County in 1810 and recorded that 1,368 gallons of wine had been made there. A staff writer for the Raleigh *Star*, who wrote about Blount's census report on January 11, 1811, was the first to call the grape variety Scuppernong.

The October 1, 1819, issue of *American Farmer* noted:

> Many farmers near Fayetteville in North Carolina have for years past drunk excellent wine of their own making from the native grape [Scuppernong] . . . Wine is made along the Cape Fear River from Fayetteville to the Sea, a distance of nearly 70 miles, and the farmers use it as freely as cider is used in New England. It is common for a farmer to make eight or ten barrels of wine annually for his own use, and many sell considerable quantities.

An early advocate of the Scuppernong grape was Sidney Weller, a graduate of Union College in Schenectady, New York, who moved to a 300-acre farm in Brinckleyville, Halifax County, North Carolina, in the late 1820s. Most of his 12-acre vineyard was planted with Scuppernong vines, but he also grew other native grape varieties, such as Norton. Weller, an energetic promoter of the Scuppernong grape, produced several thousand gallons of Scuppernong wine every year. He marketed his wine as far away as New York, New Orleans, and St. Louis. Weller's son, John, continued the winery business until the Civil War. This was the winery, purchased in 1867 by Paul Garrett's father and uncle Charles Garrett, where young Paul Garrett learned the winemaking business, beginning as a 14-year-old in 1877.

Although vintners were aware of Thomas Jefferson's failure to grow *Vitis vinifera* grapes at Monticello in Virginia, they continued to try to grow European grape varieties in America. Dr. Joseph Togno from Corsica talked to Jefferson about attempting to grow Vinifera grapes prior to the Revolutionary War; Jefferson advised against trying it. Nevertheless, Togno planted a Vinifera vineyard on a plantation near Wilmington, North Carolina, called Diccoteaux. He chose to locate in North Carolina over Virginia or Kentucky because it was a state that "flows with the milk of human kindness and Scuppernong wine."

Togno obtained his vines, "a choice collection," from the estate in France of Le Comte Odart, "proprietor of the largest collection of grapevines in the world." It is not known which Vinifera varieties he planted. Togno's failure with European varieties did not prevent him from claiming that he had successfully grown Vinifera varieties in Fauquier County, Virginia, in 1821 and 1822 on the farm of Dr. R. Peyton. Later, Togno planted Scuppernong vines.

Togno decided to educate North Carolinians on vine culture and to make the Wilmington region "the Bordeaux of America." He lectured widely in flowery style on the subject. He founded a Vine Dressers' Model School, of which he was the Principal. Unfortunately, the school did not prosper either.

In 1870, another attempt to grow Vinifera varieties was made by Eugene Morel, a native of Switzerland who had been a pupil of the highly regarded French viticultural researcher Jules Guyot. Morel settled near Ridgeway, North Carolina, where, with the help of settlers from France, he planted 100,000 cuttings of six Vinifera varieties, including Grenache and Carignane. This attempt also failed, and five years later a wiser Morel moved to Napa Valley in California, where he had a successful career.

In 1880, William McMurtrie prepared a report, *Report Upon Statistics of Grape Culture and Wine Production in the U.S.*, which ranked North Carolina second in the South in acres planted, 2,639 acres; Carteret County had 500 acres. One of the correspondents who supplied the source data was John W. Evans, scion of a family of long-term residents of Manteo, who observed: "There are two vines now living and bearing grapes on this island that are from 80 to 100 years old." Wine historians questioned whether the then-living vine, the "Mother" vine, was one of the two, and whether the original Roanoke vine actually lived that long.

The March 1, 1897, issue of *American Wine Press* noted a 1,200-acre Niagara vineyard 60 miles south of Raleigh and had an advertisement for Colonel Wharton Green's 100,000-gallon winery three miles north of Fayetteville. In 1900, the federal census of manufacturers listed wineries by state: 187 for California, 52 for Ohio, 38 for New York, 6 for Georgia, and 5 for North Carolina. That year the census reported 1,213,897 vines in North Carolina that had produced 12,344,001 pounds of grapes the previous year and from which 146,699 gallons of wine had been made. In addition, many North Carolinians made wine as a hobby.

The wine industry in Ohio, the second largest wine-producing state, was located in southern Ohio, before it moved to the shores of Lake Erie because of mildew problems along the Ohio River. Scuppernong juice was shipped from the Pamlico and Albemarle regions of North Carolina to Cincinnati by vintner Nicholas Longworth to blend with juice of Catawba grapes, his most widely grown native variety. This was done to "impart flavor and bouquet not otherwise obtainable, to his celebrated Cincinnati wines."

In the area surrounding Wilmington, North Carolina, the dominant winemakers were the family of Sol Bear. By 1902, sale of the Bears' wine extended well beyond the state. They had six salesmen on the road and an agent in New York. Their winery was a competitor of Garrett & Company in making and selling Scuppernong wine.

By 1906, the demand for Scuppernong grapes was so strong that all wineries making Scuppernong wine had to blend the juice of other grape varieties, such as Concord, with Scuppernong juice. In 1912, the Bear family built a new winery in Wilmington that produced 200,000 gallons of wine per year.

North Carolina played an important role in the first century of winemaking in the U.S. Place names on the state map, such as Catawba, Cognac, Medoc, Niagara, Tokay, and Vina Vista, indicate how widespread winegrape growing was in early North Carolina.

Early Scuppernong Growing Regions

🍇 MUSCADINES   🍇 OTHER NATIVE GRAPES

CHAPTER 3

The Scuppernong Grape Variety

"The greenish-bronze Scuppernong and its many hued relatives in the *Vitis rotundiflora* or Muscadine family are unlike any other grapes. They grow not in bunches but in clusters . . . The juice of the Scuppernong, if fermented dry, makes an amber, strong-tasting, intriguing though usually somewhat bitter wine. But when the wine is sweetened, as winemakers in Scuppernong country have always done, it becomes an exotic nectar reminiscent of fresh plums, with a musky aroma and taste entirely its own.

"The flavor of Scuppernong is so pronounced that if its wine is blended with Concord, the Scuppernong character will overwhelm and hide the foxy Concord taste. It was such a blend of Scuppernong and Concord, with California wine added, that the late Captain Paul Garrett gave the name Virginia Dare, and it was the best-selling wine in the United States during the two decades prior to Prohibition."

Leon Adams, *The Wines of America*

The fortune of Paul Garrett was to a large extent based on the sale of wine made from Scuppernong grapes. Because they are grown only in the Southern U.S., the variety is not widely known. Further description of this grape variety and its history are helpful in understanding the story of Garrett's success in the wine industry.

In 1524, Giovanni da Verrazano, a navigator from Florence, Italy, explored the Cape Fear River valley in North Carolina for the King of France. He reported many vines growing naturally there, probably the Scuppernong variety. Captain James Hawkins explored Florida and visited the Spanish settlements. He reported wild vines growing in the region and observed 20 hogsheads of wine made by the Spaniards. This wine was most likely made from Scuppernong grapes.

In 1584, Sir Walter Raleigh sent Phillip Amadas and Arthur Barlowe to explore the North Carolina coast:

> We viewed the land about us, being where we first landed very sandy and low toward the water side, but so full of grapes as the very beating and surge of the sea overflowed them, of which we found such plenty, as well there as in all places else, both on the sand and the green soil, on the hills as in the plains, as well on every little shrub, as also climbing toward the tops of high cedars, that I think in all the world the like abundance is not to be found.

The Scuppernong grape variety grows wild in the woods of the coastal plains from southern Virginia to Florida. It grows as far west as the Piedmont Region of North Carolina. The variety has a tough skin and is usually shaken from the vine, not picked as bunch grapes are. At harvest time, men walk beneath the arbored vines beating the canes with sticks, causing the grapes to drop onto sheets placed on the ground. Scuppernong fruit is not produced from the current year's growth, as other grape varieties, but on spurs that are one or more years old.

In 1817, Thomas Jefferson received some North Carolina Scuppernong wine from his son-in-law and described it as "of delicious flavor." Jefferson, who liked to promote American wines, observed that Scuppernong wine would be "distinguished on the best tables of Europe for its fine aroma and crystalline transparency." The wine that Jefferson liked was made with grapes from cultivated vineyards around Edenton and Plymouth on Albemarle Sound. The wine had been made by knowledgeable winemakers.

Unfortunately, Scuppernong wine was also made by less experienced vintners. One of their practices was to add brandy to the wine. In 1819, Congressman Nathaniel Macon sent some Scuppernong wine to Jefferson. Jefferson complained that brandy had been added to the wine and commented that it was "unworthy of being called wine."

In 1872, in *The Scuppernong Grape, Its History and Mode of Cultivation,* J. Van Buren provided advice on the proper cultivation of the Scuppernong variety:

> The Scuppernong needs but very little care or cultivation. After the vine has been planted four or five years, the shade is so perfect as to kill out the weeds and briars beneath the arbor—thus leaving nothing for the owner to do . . . The vine of the Scuppernong never needs pruning. Neither the vine, leaf, or fruit, as far as our experience extends is subject to any disease or malady; mildew is never seen upon either the vine or leaf, nor have we ever seen a rotten berry upon the vine. It is also singularly exempt from attacks of insects of all kinds . . . the foliage remains perfect and fresh until killed by the frost . . . It is the sweetest and most luscious of all the grapes we have ever met with, either native or foreign. The honeyed and delicious fragrance of the Scuppernong, when ripening, fills the air, and becomes perceptible for a considerable distance.

In addition, Van Buren observed that the productivity of Scuppernong was in a class by itself:

> The Scuppernong will produce double or treble the amount of fruit and wine per acre than any other grape in the world . . . the amount that a single vine can produce is incredible to one who has never seen the vine in bearing. Our own vines, six years transplanted, this year gave three bushels each of clear grapes. . . .

31

> Next year they will probably give at least six bushels each,
> and continue to double in quantity for several years. We
> have seen vines 10 years old yield 30 to 50 bushels per
> vine. A large vine near Mobile . . . has produced 250
> bushels of grapes in a single crop.

Van Buren's grapes yielded three gallons of juice per vine. In
the November 1867 issue of *Southern Cultivator*, P. J. Berckman of
Augusta, Georgia, cited instances of single Scuppernong vines that
produced 60 gallons of wine in one season. He cautioned that they
were exceptions all wine growers would not encounter.

R. C. Cool, manager of Southern Pines Grape Nurseries, agreed
with J. Van Buren's evaluation of the Scuppernong grape variety. In
1913, in *The Scuppernong Grape: Its Growth and Care Under
Vineyard Conditions,* he summarized his thoughts about the
Scuppernong.

> We do not believe there is another fruit combining the
> advantages that are offered to the growers of Scuppernong
> grapes. We know of no other fruit that combines the safety
> of market with low cost of production and large crops that
> are the features of the Scuppernong. The following facts
> can be proven at almost every homestead in eastern North
> Carolina:
>
> 1. There are no insect enemies of the fruit or vine and no
>   disease affecting them.
> 2. The vines require no careful and expensive pruning.
> 3. There is no danger of a late frost killing the buds.
> 4. There is no age limit to the vines.
> 5. Grapes are grown best on the cheapest land.
> 6. There is no need of expensive packages and equipment.
> 7. The vines are heavy and sure bearers.
> 8. The product has a high value and brings highest prices.
> 9. A sure market for a long term of years takes the industry
>   entirely out of the gamble class.

Paul Garrett's choice of the Scuppernong grape for his Virginia Dare wine was an obvious one. His first wineries were in North Carolina, where the prolific, easy-to-grow variety was in abundance. Virginia Dare was popular because the tastes of most wine drinkers at the time were for semisweet and sweet wine. Later, as wine tastes evolved, many wine drinkers developed a preference for semidry and dry wine.

Paul Garrett

CHAPTER 4

The Legend of Virginia Dare

"The study of written records called history should be supplement-
ed by research into myths, folklore, and legends. While the value of
history lies ever in its truth, it must bear the ideals of the people
who participated in the events narrated. Tradition was the mother of
all history, and was necessarily robed in the superstitions of the era
of which the tradition tells. History writers, jealously guarding the
truth, have striven to banish all traditions which seem colored by
fancy or even freighted with a moral lesson. These exiled traditions,
bearing the seed-germs of truth, cannot die, but, like wandering
spirits, float down the centuries enveloped in the myths of super-
stition, until, finally, embodied in romance or song, they assume a
permanent form called legend and become the heritage of a people.

"Legends are the satellites of history because they have their origin
in the same events, and the history of all countries is interspersed
with them. The Legend of the White Doe is probably the oldest and
possibly the least known of the legends which relate to the history
of the United States. It is a genuine American legend, and the facts
from which it had its origin form the first chapter in the history of
English colonization in North America."

Sallie Southall Cotten, *The White Doe: The Fate of Virginia Dare*

Sir Walter Raleigh received a charter from Queen Elizabeth I of England for the colonization of the area of North America known Virginia, which extended from Nova Scotia to Florida. Initially, England wanted to establish a base for English privateers raiding the treasure ships of Spain. Raleigh financed and organized an English colony on the Island of Roanoke, off the coast of what is now North Carolina.

Virginia Dare, the first English child born on American soil, was born on August 18, 1587, 15 days after the 117 colonists had arrived. Governor John White's daughter, Eleanor, was Virginia's mother and Ananias Dare, assistant to the Governor, was the child's father. Her baptism was the second Christian sacrament recorded in North America. The first recorded baptism was that of the Indian chief, Manteo, who was honored for his service in getting settled.

Before Virginia was a year old, Governor White had to return to England to obtain critically needed supplies. When White left the colony, it was comprised of 87 men, 17 women, and 11 children. Upon his arrival in England, he found the country at war and threatened by the Spanish armada. Queen Elizabeth extended his stay, and he was not able to sail for the colony at Roanoke until 1590. Upon his return, he could find no trace of the settlement. It became known as the "Lost Colony."

An agreement had been made that if the colony had to leave Roanoke Island, they would carve their destination on a tree. If they had to relocate because of being attacked, they were to carve a Maltese cross as a distress signal over the carving of the new location. Governor White found no sign of distress carved on tree, just the word "Croatoan."

All of the dwellings had been dismantled, which led White to believe that their departure had been planned. The fate of the lost colony is unknown to this day. Many folktales grew out of the colony's mysterious disappearance, including one that they had become part of an Indian tribe with a name similar to Croatoan.

According to the most popular legend of Virginia Dare, Chief Manteo was returning from a fishing expedition when he saw that the colonists were being attacked by a hostile Indian tribe and led them to safety. He transported them by canoe down the Pimlico River to his village at Hatteras, where they were accepted into his tribe as brothers and sisters.

The February 12, 1885, edition of the Fayetteville *Observer* published its opinion of the fate of the lost colony:

> The people we call the Croatoan Indians (though they do not recognize that name as that of a tribe, but only a village, and that they were Tuscaroras), were always friendly to the whites; and finding them destitute and despairing of ever receiving aid from England, persuaded them to leave the island, and go to the mainland.

According to legend, Virginia Dare was a wonder to the Indians because of her fair skin and blond hair. When she reached maturity, many braves sought her hand in marriage, but she held off in choosing a mate. She was loved by Okisko, a young brave, and by Chico, an old, evil medicine man. Virginia was kind to Chico, but it was obvious that his ardor was not returned.

In one version of the legend, Chico turned Virginia into a white doe. Okisko asked Wanaudon, a medicine man, to make a magic arrow that would restore Virginia to her human form. A deer hunt was organized. Chico took his magic arrow, but another hunter, Wanchese, son of Chief Wanchese, had a silver arrow, which he knew was required to kill a white deer.

Both braves shot their arrows at the same time, and both struck the white doe. The doe turned into Virginia, who died before their eyes with the arrows piercing her heart. She was was buried by Okisko.

Okisko visited her grave frequently and one day found a tiny shoot with small leaves growing out of it. He tended it, and it grew into a grapevine with blood-red juice. Okisko drank the juice and felt that he had been reunited with Virginia. This story was intended to explain the source of the red Scuppernong grape, which had been known previously only as a white grape.

In another version of the legend, when Chico's love was not returned by Virginia, he vowed that if she would not marry him, she would not marry anyone. Chico lured Virginia to Roanoke Island, where, with the assistance of the power of sea nymphs, she was turned to a white doe.

The white doe became the leader of all deer on Roanoke Island. Wherever this extraordinary creature went, others followed. Many hunters attempted to slay her, but they were unsuccessful. Eventually, in addition to being a challenge for hunters, she became a growing legend.

A great hunt was organized, and all the braves renewed their efforts. The successful hunter would be presented with high honors. Wanchese, the son of Chief Wanchese, who had traveled to England, had with him on the hunt the silver-tipped arrow that Queen Elizabeth had presented to his father. Young Wanchese believed that the arrow had magical powers that would help him bring down the quarry.

Wanchese sighted the white doe, took careful aim, and fired the silver-tipped arrow. The doe fell to the ground, and the young brave advanced to claim his prize. Any joy in his accomplishment was lost when he heard the dying doe say with her last breath, faintly but clearly, "Virginia Dare."

Because the name, Virginia Dare, symbolized wholesomeness and purity, as well as new beginnings, promise, and hope, Paul Garrett chose it as the brand name for Garrett & Company's Scuppernong wine.

CHAPTER 5

Overcoming Obstacles

"Life affords no higher pleasure than of surmounting difficulties, passing from one step of success to another, forming new wishes, and seeing them gratified. He that labors in any great or laudable undertaking has his fatigues first supported by hope and then by joy."

Samuel Johnson

When we think of an individual who is successful in business, we tend to think of a person who started with a small operation, worked hard, and expanded the business until it was large and profitable. Generally, we think of steady growth that was virtually inevitable. Most businessmen and businesswomen experience problems and obstacles along the way that must be overcome, in some cases for the survival of the business.

The path to success is rarely smooth, due to circumstances that cannot be controlled, such as social conditions, the political environment, and competition. The personal characteristic of resilience is critical to the success of a business. This was certainly true during the career of Paul Garrett, as illustrated by the following examples from Garrett's *Reminiscences.*

When Paul Garrett dropped out of school to assist his uncle, Charles Garrett, with running his winery, he moved in with this aunt Mary and his uncle to learn the business. He worked long hours, five or six days a week over the next seven years, keeping the books, handling the correspondence, filling orders, and making wine.

After Garrett had worked seven years at the winery, his uncle Charles became seriously ill. He called his wife, Mary, and son-in-law, Spooner Harrison, to his bedside and insisted that, under no circumstances, should Garrett be permitted to leave the company, and that he was to be given a 25% interest in the winery. Unfortunately, Harrison, a heavy drinker who had not contributed much to the business, had other ideas. He planned to take sole charge of the winery. Harrison, under the influence of alcohol, called Garrett into his office and told him to look for another job.

Garrett replied that he would, except that his aunt Mary had made him promise not to leave the winery. He said that until his aunt relieved him of his promise, he planned to stay. The next several weeks were contentious. Finally, Garrett convinced his aunt that operation of the business could not continue as it was. After having made significant contributions to the winery working for his uncle Charles, Garrett was forced to look for other employment.

Sy and June Wright of Little Rock, Arkansas, were agents for C. W. Garrett & Company and were the winery's top salesmen. Garrett had worked with them on numerous occasions when they visited the Halifax County winery to settle their accounts and to place orders for the coming year. Although Garrett was still a young man, they respected him and, when they heard that he was available, asked him to open an office for them in Little Rock.

Garrett moved to Little Rock and immediately got his first taste of the legal profession and politics. The State of Arkansas had passed a law to encourage grape growing in the state that authorized the unlimited sale of wine made from fruit grown in Arkansas, free from restrictions on either the manufacturer or an agent appointed by the manufacturer. The Wright brothers had contracted with the owner of a 25-acre vineyard in Pine Bluff, Arkansas, to supply them with Scuppernong grapes to make wine. The brothers planned to press grapes from out of state to blend with the home-grown grapes and to sell the wine as Arkansas wine.

Garrett declined to participate in activities that were clearly against the law and tendered his resignation. This was an early indication of Garrett's integrity. The brothers understood Garrett's concern about breaking the law, which subsequently was found to be unconstitutional. They countered with the offer of a salary that was ten times more than Garrett had ever earned, raised $75,000 and placed it in a local bank in his name, rented a store on the most prominent corner of Little Rock, and directed him to open a store there. Sy and June had a high regard for young Garrett's abilities.

Garrett declined their offer; they waved to him as they left on the next train. The only people Garrett knew in Little Rock were his banker and the bank's lawyer, Judge Saunders, considered the best constitutional lawyer in Arkansas.

Garrett spent his spare time reading law books in Judge Saunders's office. He read about interstate commerce law and noted that it applied to the Wright brothers' situation. The law guaranteed equity of trade among the states. Garrett asked the judge why, if the State of Arkansas permitted wine to be made and sold in the state, they were allowed, under interstate commerce law, to prevent wine from other states to be sold. Judge Saunders realized that the Wright brothers had a valid case and asked them to cut their selling trips short and return to Little Rock to discuss it.

Judge Saunders met Garrett and the Wright brothers and told them he thought that he could obtain a favorable ruling in their case. However, it would take four months for the Supreme Court to act on it. The brothers asked Garrett to sell wine on the road between Little Rock and Texas for the next several months. Sy traveled with him by train to Texarkana, coaching him along the way about selling on the road. Garrett had never had a drink of whiskey, nor had he never been in a saloon. He was about to have his eyes opened.

The first saloon Garrett visited was in Blossom Prairie, Texas. The proprietor, a lanky, unkempt man with a drooping, stained mustache, was sitting in front of the fireplace. He did not get up, and he seemed surprised at Garrett's youthful appearance, showing none of the bearing or assurance of the usual traveling salesman. Garrett introduced himself and told the proprietor that he was selling wine. He had no business card, but he handed the proprietor a list of wines that he sold.

The proprietor's response was one that Garrett was to hear over and over: "I don't sell no wine, Sonny. I wouldn't sell a drink in a month; in fact, I don't remember that I ever heard a call for wine. Folks in this country want red 'likker'—the stronger, the better." Wishing that he was back in North Carolina, Garrett described the Scuppernong grape and noted that some of the finest wine in the world was made from it. Garrett offered the proprietor a sample taste of the wine from a small vial that he carried with him. The proprietor's kindly manner seemed to express sympathy, if not interest.

Garrett explained that he shipped wine in barrels, half-barrels, and ten-gallon kegs. The proprietor ordered a barrel of one wine, then another, and another, without asking for the price of a barrel, which was from $40 to $50. Garrett looked around the small, empty saloon, with no accumulated stock, and wondered about the man's ability to pay. After calculating that the order would cost from $200 to $300, Garrett suggested that since the proprietor had never sold wine before, it might be advisable to start with half-barrels and ten-gallon kegs so that he could determine which varieties sold best. This reduced the order to about $100.

Garrett's greatest objection to selling wine was the understanding that when a salesman entered a saloon, he was expected to treat the customers and to be the heaviest drinker himself. In this first saloon, Garrett had admitted to the proprietor that this was his first time away from home and his first visit to a saloon, and that he had never had a drink of whiskey in his young life. Garrett offered to buy the proprietor a whiskey. The proprietor replied, "I don't often take a drink myself, Sonny, and let me tell you something—if you haven't ever took a drink of whiskey, don't start." Garrett considered this the best advice that he ever received.

The proprietor added, "You don't have to drink, sonny, you knows your business, and you can sell goods without taking a drink." Garrett was nearly overwhelmed to hear this and asked, "Do you mean to tell me I can go into a saloon and solicit business, and even if given an order, I don't have to drink?" When the proprietor responded, "Shore you don't." Garrett seized his hand and shook it with a sigh of relief. That customer stayed on their books for many years and always paid his bills promptly.

Texas was part of the wild West in those days. Most men carried a gun, and shootings, sometime fatal ones, occurred in saloons. As soon as trouble started, Garrett left the premises. Occasionally, he would be cornered by a man who took offense at Garrett's refusal to take a drink, but he managed to avoid trouble.

After months on the road, Sy Wright invited Garrett to meet him to go over the books and total the orders. When Sy totaled his own orders, he was pleased to see that he had earned commissions of $800 to $900. Garrett reviewed his sales and noted that in calculating commissions, he had included only orders that had been approved for shipment. Garrett's commissions over the same period of time totalled $1,870, more than twice the commissions earned by Sy. Sy was impressed. In addition, Garrett had commissions of over $700 that were awaiting credit approval on his orders. Sy told him that if he continued to do as well in his sales territory, they would make him a partner.

As the Wrights' lawyer, Judge Saunders, had assured them, they were in a position to sell wine made in North Carolina in Arkansas. Garrett attended the presentation of their case before the Supreme Court of Arkansas in Little Rock. The decision of the Chief Justice was virtually a duplicate of the brief submitted by Judge Saunders. Garrett signed the contract with C. W. Garrett & Company to supply the wines.

Garrett was assigned to northern Arkansas, one of the Wright brothers marketed in the western part of the state, and the other was responsible for southern Arkansas. By the end of the first week, they had established 100 agencies in the state. Garrett worked the bottling operation 18 hours a day and did a substantial business. He displayed his diversity by serving as office manager, marketer for northern Arkansas, and bottling supervisor.

On one occasion in Rocky Point, Arkansas, Garrett was asked to take an order out in the country, accompanied by a driver. The building was well lit that night, the stove had a roaring fire, and about a dozen men in the bar were playing poker. The card players had obviously been drinking heavily. Garrett told the men that he was selling wine legally in the state through agencies. One of the men accused Garrett of being a revenue officer or a detective. Garrett told him that he was not and showed the man the contract that documented that he could sell wine legally.

Realizing that he could not convince the man that his credentials were genuine, Garrett began to edge toward the door. However, the man kept himself between Garrett and the door. Garrett was a husky young man and did not fear taking on the man. Unfortunately, the man was armed, and he wasn't. The driver came up behind Garrett and tried to press a revolver into his hand. Garrett did not take the pistol from the driver but pressed the man back to the door. The man called out, "Come on, boys, this chap is a revenuer or a detective; let's lynch him." As they approached, the other men cried out, "Let's ride him out on a rail."

Garrett pushed them out of the way and ran for it, followed by his driver. As Garrett and the driver ran from the building, many shots rang out. Fortunately, it was a stormy night, and they made it back to their buggy safely.

The agencies that the Wright brothers had established as part of the Standard Wine Company to market wine in Arkansas thrived, keeping Garrett busy with bottling activities. When the stock of 250,000 gallons of wine contracted earlier was almost depleted, the Standard Wine Company decided to order stocks of California wine.

Unfortunately, changes were occurring. When Garrett started calling on saloons to sell wine, the old-fashioned saloon keeper was usually an Irishman with a big heart. His patrons were his friends, and he would not serve a drunken man. Things began to change with the entry of large breweries doing a national business. The modest saloon was replaced by a fancy bar with pool tables. The hired barkeeper was motivated to earn as much as he could from his customers, including those who were inebriated. These changes made the saloon business a target for reformers.

Also, some of the companies selling out-of-state wine in Arkansas, including some from Missouri and Ohio, were using the worst class of bottlers. The Standard Wine Company suffered from guilt by association. When the Anti-Saloon League went after the wine distributors, they went after all of them, including the Wright brothers, even though they were operating under the law.

Anti-alcohol sentiment was running high in Arkansas. The goal of the local judge in Camden was to drive all wineries out of the state by persuading the Governor to call a special session of the legislature. The Wright brothers realized it was a battle that eventually would be lost. They closed the Standard Wine Company in Arkansas and moved to Memphis, Tennessee. This was Garrett's first of many experiences with aroused public sentiment.

Garrett had made an agreement with June Wright that he would be manager of the Memphis office and would not have to travel. The stock from Medoc Vineyard was nearly exhausted, so Garrett went to California to look for another source of wine. He signed a contract with the San Gabriel Wine Company and returned to North Carolina to marry his childhood sweetheart, Sadie Walton Harrison.

June Wright reneged on his agreement that Garrett would not have to travel. June asked him to alternate months of travel with him. Without consulting his brother, June said that if Garrett would not go on the road every other month, he could either buy the company or sell his share. Garrett could not afford to buy the company, so he elected to sell his share.

When Sy Wright heard of this, he begged Garrett to stay and agreed that he would not have to go on the road. Garrett realized that this arrangement would cause hard feelings between the brothers, so he returned to North Carolina with no job prospects. At that time, the Memphis concern was the exclusive agency for all Medoc Vineyard wine.

Shortly after returning to North Carolina, Garrett received a call from Spooner Harrison, manager of C. W. Garrett & Company, which included Medoc Vineyard. Harrison told him that between the time that Garrett had left Memphis and his arrival in North Carolina, Harrison had broken with the Wright brothers. Harrison offered Garrett the exclusive selling agency for the firm.

Garrett prepared a contract in which he agreed to sell not only all wines currently produced, but also all that C. W. Garrett & Company might produce or control in the future. No commissions were involved. Garrett was to pay the company a flat rate for their wines, thus ensuring them a guaranteed, ample profit. All collection of payments on the invoices was done by them, but they gave Garrett the right to supervise the preparation of the wine. Harrison signed the contract.

Garrett's sales the first month were beyond his expectations. He was on the road for 30 days, and he worked long hours. He received no reply to his letters to Harrison, informing him of his success. When he arrived home, he went to the winery to review the books to see if his orders had been properly recorded. Garrett was not permitted to see the books. Harrison told Garrett that he was going to cancel the contract; he was making too much money: $4,000 profit for 30 days of selling. Harrison told him that he was worth only $100 per month and expenses.

Garrett had paid all of his own expenses on the road and asked to be reimbursed for them. Harrison told him that he had no money and did not owe him anything until the invoices for his orders were paid. Garrett returned to his wife with anxious feelings. Harrison was her brother and had married Garrett's first cousin, so he was faced with serious family conflicts.

Garrett had not consulted an attorney in drawing up his contract, but he went to one now. After reviewing Garrett's earnings over the last several years, the attorney advised him to go home and do nothing. He assured Garrett that he would have no difficulty collecting $40,000 to $50,000 a year under the simple contract that Garrett had drawn up.

Garrett was not satisfied doing nothing and went to the offices of C. W. Garrett & Company to plead for a continuation of his contract. Garrett told Harrison that he was going on another selling trip. When Harrison told him that they would not fill his orders, Garrett reminded him that this would be a breach of contract and that his lawyer assured him that he could collect. Harrison decided to take advantage in a clause in the contract: that the contract could only be voided by the sale of the winery. He began to negotiate with a potential purchaser from Boston.

Garrett decided to go into business for himself. He made a new arrangement with Harrison. Since Garrett had not been able to collect any money from the winery, he agreed to take goods from them in payment of their debt to him. Garrett founded Garrett & Company and opened a warehouse in Littleton, North Carolina. After two or three of Garrett's road trips, Harrison said that he would no longer fill Garrett's orders for goods, thus further aggravating the tension in their relationship.

Having booked many orders for wine, Garrett looked for another source. He visited the Urbana Wine Company in Hammondsport, New York, in the Finger Lakes Region, which made wines similar to those he was selling. He contracted Urbana Wine Company to ship two or three carloads of wine, principally Catawba and Port, to his warehouse in North Carolina.

Garrett continued to try to reestablish a working relationship with C. W. Garrett & Company, without success. Unfortunately, Harrison maintained the false position that the winery had been sold, in order to negate Garrett's contract.

Within a short period of time, Garrett's father passed away, and then his young wife died of influenza. Garrett moved to Weldon, North Carolina, in a region where he knew he could find an ample supply of grapes. Garrett did not remarry until 1896, when he married Evelyn Edwards. The local newspaper described her as "one of Weldon's loveliest and most popular young ladies."

Garrett recruited two brothers-in-law and a cousin, who lived in Weldon, to join Garrett & Company. Garrett's father had appointed him executor of his estate. This responsibility was very demanding of Garrett's time, and he turned over the running of Garrett & Company to his brothers-in-law and his cousin.

When he had settled his father's estate, Garrett returned to the winery and found that not only had his relatives made no profit, they had lost the $20,000 to $30,000 that he had left with them. Garrett was virtually broke. Within six months, however, Garrett had gained back his losses.

From time to time, Garrett had to assert himself to achieve his business goals. On one occasion, he needed more money than his local bank could afford to lend him to expand his business. He was a director of the bank and frequently borrowed more than the bank's total capital.

Garrett had a good friend in Richmond, Virginia, who was a large stockholder and director of the First National Bank there. He suggested that Garrett form a corporation and have the directors sign the notes for the loan jointly. Garrett asked three of his employees to become directors of the corporation, with 10% of the stock each, and to sign the notes. They refused to sign. Garrett told them that they must either sign the notes or lose their jobs.

Sugar is one of the required ingredients of wine. Garrett's uncle Charles had always bought American Sugar Refining Company sugar from a wholesaler in Richmond. Garrett needed a carload of sugar for his ongoing winemaking efforts. He requested $5,000 credit from the wholesaler in Richmond, offering notes as collateral, and was turned down. The wholesale firm knew about Garrett's break with C. W. Garrett & Company and refused to accept his notes as collateral. The manager of the wholesale company told Garrett that he was an upstart for quitting his previous employer, that he had no chance of succeeding against his old firm, and that he would soon be a failure. Garrett left the wholesaler's offices in a depressed frame of mind.

As Garrett walked down the street, he saw a sign for D. A. Saunders & Company. The name sounded familiar to him, so he went into their offices. He was desperate and did not want to go home empty handed. Garrett showed Saunders his collateral, consisting of notes and mortgages, and was told that they would consider his request and get back to him.

Garrett returned to Weldon and received an envelope in the mail the next day from Saunders. Assuming that Saunders was rejecting his request and returning his collateral documents, he did not even open the envelope.

Later in the day, a railroad employee came into Garrett's office to tell him that he had two carloads of sugar out on the tracks and asked him what he wanted done with it. Garrett, who had asked for only one carload of sugar, tore open the envelope and read: "After considering your proposition of this afternoon, I am returning the papers you left with me as collateral and take pleasure in stating that I have authorized a shipping account on our books for you to the extent of $10,000."

Eight years later, when Garrett was undergoing a substantial expansion of his business by building a new plant and adding inventory, he again went to Saunders for the necessary capital. Saunders told him to construct the facility and when he needed money to come to him and he would obtain it from his bank. When construction was almost completed and Garrett had to purchase the necessary cooperage, he visited Saunders to tell him that he would need $50,000 from his bank.

Saunders was astounded to hear that Garrett wanted his bank to loan him that much money. He asked Garrett where he had been for the last several months. Garrett replied that he had been hard at work with his nose to the grindstone. Saunders informed him that banks were not making loans to anybody, unless backed by securities such as United States bonds.

Garrett asked what to do, since he had spent all of his money and that he was on his way to Cincinnati to buy cooperage and urgently needed to borrow $50,000. When Saunders told him to go home and shut down his business, Garrett told him that it would ruin him. Saunders offered to cover his existing debts, and told him there was nothing else that he could do until after the next Presidential election. Furthermore, he said that, in his opinion, if William Jennings Bryan was elected, the country was in for long-term economic problems. Saunders stormed out of the office but returned to ask Garrett what he was going to do. Garrett told him that in spite of what appeared to be certain failure, he was going ahead with his expansion project.

Saunders said that he admired Garrett's nerve more than he respected his judgement. Then he asked what the $50,000 was required for. Garrett told him that it was needed for sugar and cooperage. Saunders turned on him and asked why he hadn't mentioned that one of the main needs was for sugar, which he could provide in unlimited quantities. He said he could ship 10 or 20 or 50 thousand barrels. A relieved Garrett proceeded to Cincinnati to purchase the necessary cooperage. The economy was down, and the cooperage company was having a poor year. They provided Garrett with unlimited credit. He went from nearly having to shut down his plant to having one of his best years in business until that time.

As Garrett's business expanded, it competed for customers and suppliers with C. W. Garrett & Company, particularly since Garrett owned only a few small vineyards and purchased grapes from thousands of grape growers throughout the coastal region of North Carolina and Virginia. Other wineries, observing Garrett's success with the Scuppernong grape, began to offer Scuppernong wine, some of which was inferior.

One of the C. W. Garrett & Company salesmen assigned to the Texas territory, always a popular region for Scuppernong wine, produced a circular issued by that winery implying that Garrett was an impostor and a renegade. To support that claim, the company circulated a document signed by Thomas Harrison, Chairman of the Board of Commissioners of Halifax County, North Carolina, alleging that Garrett was using unfair practices to steal the business of a competitor who was responsible for his being in business. Garrett responded by challenging the accuracy of the circulars and branding Harrison as a political outlaw.

C. W. Garrett & Company's attorney, who had tried to break the earlier contract with Paul Garrett by a fraudulent sale of the winery, took the issue to arbitration. Paul Garrett was sued for libel. After a lengthy, expensive court battle, he won a decisive legal victory.

These examples of Garrett's resilience along his path to success illustrate that achievement of one's goals is often not easy. Many individuals with less drive would have given up in dealing with the challenges faced by Garrett. He overcame many obstacles and moved on to become the dean of American winemakers and a multimillionaire.

Garrett & Company Winery, Weldon, North Carolina

Garrett Family—Paul, Evelyn, Daughters, and Governess

CHAPTER 6

A Failed Attempt to Swindle Paul Garrett

"A lesson well learned is demonstrated by the remarks made by a man who, at one time in the past, lost a great deal of money in a gold mine speculation. When asked by a friend to define the term, 'bonanza,' he said, 'A bonanza is a hole in the ground owned by a champion liar.'"

Edmund Fuller, ed., *Thesaurus of Anecdotes*

Paul Garrett had many strong personal characteristics. One of them was his ability to spot a swindler when he saw one. In another fascinating tale from *Reminiscences*, Garrett described how he foiled a swindler. A stranger walked into Garrett's winery office in Weldon, North Carolina, with no appointment and without checking in with the receptionist. Garrett looked up from his work to see a heavyset man, just under six feet tall, with a face that showed unusual strength. The man asked Garrett if he was Mr. Garrett. He answered that he was and asked the visitor what he wanted. He said that he wanted to talk privately with Garrett.

By this time, the visitor was getting on Garrett's nerves. They went out onto the front porch. The man asked Garrett if he was P. Garrett; he was looking for Peter Garrett. The stranger had been told that his old friend, Peter Garrett, had moved to Weldon. Garrett replied in a somewhat uncivil tone that he had guessed wrong; his name was Paul Garrett.

The stranger, who still had not introduced himself, was one of the most competent actors that Garrett had ever seen. He assumed an injured air, begged his pardon for intruding, and said that he was really in distress. He told of childhood hardships with both of his parents dead and of moving to cattle country in the far West and becoming associated with cowboys and Indians. Years ago, the visitor had formed a strong friendship with young Peter Garrett. They were close friends for two or three years and then went in different directions. They swore that if either of them ran into good fortune, they would share it with the other. The stranger fell in with a tribe of Indians and eventually became one of their chiefs.

At this stage of the discussion, Garrett was beginning to become suspicious of this story of the wild West. After becoming a confidant of the tribe, the stranger said he was shown one of the richest gold mines in the West. The tribe visited the mine once a year to obtain nuggets of gold, digging with crude methods.

The stranger showed Garrett a clipping from an Albuquerque, New Mexico, newspaper about a tribe of Indians, headed by Chief Gomez, who was traveling to the East with him to purchase machinery for the tribe's gold mine, allowing them to dig more efficiently. Unfortunately, on the trip east, the stranger and Gomez had fallen in with some shrewd swindlers and had been relieved of most of the money they had brought with them for the purchase of equipment. The visitor described his fellow traveler, Gomez, as a dumb Indian who was tired of traveling and wanted to return to his tribe, so the stranger had left the chief at a camp in the woods near Greensboro.

Gomez and his companion also planned to visit the mint in Philadelphia, where they were going to dispose of two bars of gold that they were carrying with them. The visitor unwrapped a piece of cloth containing two gold nuggets that he said were worth $100,000. He showed them to Garrett; they had the appearance of real gold.

What the visitor did not know was that Garrett had some knowledge of gold. In between leaving the C. W. Garrett & Company winery, and hiring on with Sy and June Wright in Little Rock, he had lived briefly with his father in Kings Mountain, North Carolina. Garrett had secured a position in a gold mine several miles from Kings Mountain.

The Wright brothers wrote many letters attempting to convince Garrett to work for them in Arkansas. Garrett reviewed the letters with his employer, Major Horton, president of the gold mine. Horton realized the rare opportunity that Garrett was being offered in Little Rock and suggested that Garrett take it. His father also advised him not to lose this chance for advancement. Although his employment at the gold mine was brief, Garrett had become familiar with gold and gold mining.

Garrett realized that he was dealing with a real operator. He was surprised that his suspicions had not been detected by the visitor. Garrett wondered if he had really fooled this scam artist, or if the man was just trying to project his power to convince. The visitor asked Garrett to join him in exploiting the mine and told him how nice it would be to get away from the cares of running a business. Garrett reminded him that he was not Peter Garrett. The visitor said that he was sure his friend would not mind substituting a competent person like Garrett to take charge of this wonderful mine. After all, he had made a diligent effort to find Peter Garrett.

Garrett was sufficiently aware of the hold this man had on him that he took a pin from his lapel and stuck in into his leg to throw off the man's hypnotic spell. He suggested that Garrett join him in visiting Gomez in the woods near Greensboro. Garrett wondered how much longer he could conceal his feelings that he was observing a swindler. Outwardly, Garrett indicated that he was warming up to the visions of ease and travel that untold riches would bring.

The visitor explained that the trip west would cost Garrett nothing and even if he decided not to join in managing the gold mine, all of his expenses would be paid. The visitor pulled a roll of bills out of his wallet and asked Garrett to count it. Garrett counted $800.00, all of which appeared to be real money. The visitor insisted that Garrett take the money as assurance that his bills would be paid. Garrett took only $10.00 to pay for his trip to Greensboro. The stranger then took a larger roll of money, consisting of bills of large denomination, from his pocket and again insisted that Garrett count it. It contained $40,000 to $50,000 in questionable money.

Garrett told him that he couldn't possibly accompany him to Greensboro because he was looking at property in Norfolk, Virginia, the next day. Because North Carolina had a strong Anti-Saloon League that made it difficult for wineries to operate in the state, Garrett was moving the winery to Virginia, which at the time was more tolerant of alcohol. He told the man that if Gomez was interested in Garrett joining them, the visitor should send Garrett a telegram in Norfolk and he would visit Greensboro the following day.

Garrett went into town, picked up his mail, described his situation to a friend, and asked for his assistance. The friend was an ex-Confederate soldier who worked for the revenue service. Garrett asked his friend to review the situation with Deputy Revenue Collector Patterson in Greensboro. Garrett notified Patterson by telegram that he would be in Greensboro the following day. Patterson obtained the assistance of the sheriff in their endeavor.

The miner met Garrett at the train station the next day. At dinner at the miner's hotel, Garrett was told of the location of Gomez's camp at Buffalo Creek. After dinner, they made arrangements to rent a horse and buggy to transport them to Gomez's camp. At the hotel, Garrett had a private conversation with his friend, who told him that the local magistrate did not think that they had sufficient evidence to issue a warrant for the arrest of the men. Garrett told his friend where Gomez was.

On the way to the camp, the miner told Garrett that no matter what his decision was, Gomez had decided to sell out and return home. He would sell his interest for $100,000; the miner suggested that he and Garrett each put up $50,000 and become equal partners in the lucrative gold mine. Garrett didn't agree but told him that it would take him several days to raise $50,000.

The miner said that his objective in coming to the camp was not only to talk with Gomez about the sale of his interest in the mine, but also to have Garrett bore into some gold bars to prove to him that they were real. The miner had brought along a brace and bit and a set of scales. He removed the wrapping from two bars of brilliantly gilded brass, each about two inches by four inches and 18 inches long, and weighing 75 to 80 pounds. Garrett was about to bore into one of the bars with the brace and bit, when someone called out from the woods, "throw up your hands."

Gomez leveled a pistol at the sheriff, who had accompanied Patterson. The sheriff said, "Drop the gun and throw up your hands or I will put daylight through you." When the Indian dropped his gun, the miner made a move for his, which was in a holster on his belt. Garrett grabbed the man's wrist in a firm grip and pressed his own pistol into the miner's stomach. The surprised miner asked, "What does this mean?" Garrett held onto the miner's wrist until Patterson came over and took the miner's arm. The miner asked to see the warrant for his arrest. Patterson showed him his badge and told him he didn't need a warrant, and that he would let him know later what the charges were.

The miner took a card from one of his pockets and attempted to grind it into the dirt. The sheriff retrieved the card and found on it the name of an alleged employee of the Philadelphia mint who was staying at a local hotel. This associate, who was willing to provide a certificate that the content of the two bars of brass were 22-carat gold, was arrested as well.

Patterson and the sheriff took Garrett aside and explained that the leading attorneys in Greensboro insisted that no crime had been committed unless he had been robbed of some money. They suggested that he hurry back to Greensboro and engage an attorney to document the fact that the men had attempted to swindle him. Garrett had recently spoken with his own attorney about the law of conspiracy. Nevertheless, it took him hours to convince the Greensboro attorneys that conspiracy between two or more people to commit a crime was in itself a crime. With misgivings, the attorneys agreed to handle the case for him.

Within 24 hours of the arrest, 12 lawyers from New York and Chicago arrived in Greensboro to represent their clients in the Superior Court case. Most of Greensboro's attorneys were retained as prosecutors. The $40,000 to $50,000 was used to pay their fees. Soon victims of the swindlers began to arrive from all over the country. The trio claimed to be modern-day Robin Hoods—stealing from the rich to give to the poor. They were confident that they would not be convicted of the charges against them.

The men were not only convicted but were given the maximum sentence under North Carolina law for criminal conspiracy to defraud: 10 years in prison. After their conviction, telegrams poured into the Governor's office asking for clemency, and every one of Garrett's intimate friends was approached with offers to pay any amount to induce him to sign a petition of clemency for the convicted men. Garrett told them that he harbored no resentment against the men, but that their pardon was in the hands of the Governor.

The man who had played the part of the Indian chief, a minor role, was eventually pardoned by the Governor. The alleged associate of the Philadelphia mint, who was really a bookmaker, died in prison. Hawley, the miner, served his full sentence of 10 years.

Empire State Winery, Penn Yan, New York

Paul Garrett

Garrett & Company Winery, Penn Yan, New York, later Boordy Winery

CHAPTER 7

Pre-Prohibition and Prohibition

"For the fourteen years of Prohibition, the wine industry, like the beer trade and the distilled spirits trade, was legally ended. As it turned out, the measure intended to kill Demon Rum in this country managed to give it hardly more than a flesh wound. Liquor of all kinds continued to be made by one means or another, and people, perhaps in larger numbers than ever before, continued to drink liquor of all kinds. Yet the interruption to the normal growth and functioning of winegrowing in this country had disruptive and destructive effects that are still being felt and will continue to be felt as long as one can foresee."

Thomas Pinney, *A History of Wine in America from the Beginnings to Prohibition*

Early advocates of temperance in drinking advocated not so much abstinence in drinking, but moderation. One of Aristotle's doctrines was "nothing too much." Poet John Milton praised wine. In 1784, Philadelphia physician Benjamin Rush published an early treatise on the subject, *An Inquiry Into the Effects of Spiritous Liquors Upon the Human Body.* By "spirituous liquors," he meant rum and whiskey, which were inexpensive and plentiful in his day. Rush did not advise against the temperate use of wine; in fact, he prescribed it for health and longevity. He observed: "It must be a bad heart, indeed, that is not rendered more cheerful and more generous by a few glasses of wine."

The early temperance movement was concerned only with hard liquor and advocated "light wine, beer, and happiness." Temperance gained momentum slowly in the U.S., beginning with the 1816 Indiana law banning the sale of alcoholic beverages on Sunday, which made no exception for wine. In 1826, the American Temperance Society was founded in Boston. By 1832, the Society had 31 auxiliaries in North Carolina.

During the 1840s, many towns and counties in the East and Midwest went Dry in the States of Georgia, Indiana, Iowa, Michigan, New Hampshire, and New York. In 1843, Portland, Maine, was the first city to vote itself Dry. Frances Willard founded the Women's Christian Temperance Union (WCTU) in 1874. Entire states began to go Dry, beginning with Kansas in 1880 and Iowa in 1882, followed by Georgia, Oklahoma, Mississippi, North Carolina, Tennessee, West Virginia, and Virginia.

The Anti-Saloon League, founded in 1895, became the leader in the politics of the Dry cause and in the dissemination of propaganda advocating temperance. The Anti-Saloon League became the driving force of the Dry campaign. Politically, the league was extremely flexible and pursued whatever policy was likely to work in a particular circumstance.

Late in the nineteenth century, the popularity of prohibition increased nationwide. Nevertheless, production of commercial wines in the United States expanded considerably during the first two decades of the twentieth century. In 1900, 24 million gallons were produced, which increased to 39 million gallons in 1918.

In 1903, the rural districts of North Carolina became Dry, and beginning in 1909, North Carolina law prohibited the manufacture and sale of intoxicating liquors. Clarence Poe cited three reasons in the *Progressive Farmer* for this trend in the South:

- lack of a large foreign population
- predominance of church influences
- necessity of keeping liquor from [individuals] of the baser sort

Garrett realized that he had to move his wine production facilities out of North Carolina; nevertheless, he retained ownership of his properties in the state. In 1903, he moved his winery and headquarters to Norfolk, Virginia. Norfolk was good choice because it was a trucking and rail center and had manufacturers of crates and cooperage, one of which produced over 1,000 barrels a day. Unfortunately, although Virginia was the last southern state to go Dry, the Anti-Saloon League was very active and sponsored laws that prevented wineries from selling their wines locally.

By 1910, Garrett's first winery in Penn Yan, New York, Empire State Winery, was operational. Later, he sold this facility to Frank Hallett, who had been his winemaker in Penn Yan.

In 1911, Garrett purchased 2,000 acres in San Bernardino County, California, and established the Mission Vineyard and Winery in Cucamonga. Nearby were the substantial holdings of Secondo Guasti's huge Italian Vineyard Company and the Padre Vineyard Company, which were known for their Port wine.

In 1912, Garrett sold his facilities in Norfolk and moved his headquarters to Penn Yan in the Finger Lakes Region. He was familiar with the region from his purchases of Finger Lakes wine to sell and for blending with his Garrett & Company wine.

By 1914, 33 states had gone Dry. In the opinion of Will Rogers, "Many folks staggered to the polls to vote Dry." On January 16, 1919, the Eighteenth Amendment (the Prohibition Amendment) to the Constitution was ratified. Unfortunately, wine was grouped with hard liquor as "intoxicating" by the Volstead Act that became law on October 28, 1919. President Wilson had proposed defining as "intoxicating" drinks containing more than 10 to 12 percent alcohol. The wine industry would have been saved; however, Wilson's veto was overridden by Congress. Many wineries went out of business.

Paul Garrett

The New York *Daily News* published a list of dos and don'ts:

1. You may drink intoxicating liquor in your own home or in the home of a bona fide friend.
2. You may buy intoxicating liquor on a bona fide medical prescription of a doctor. A pint can be bought every 10 days.
3. You may call any place you live permanently as your home. If you have more than one home, you may keep a stock of liquor in each.
4. You may keep liquor in any storage room or club locker, provided the storage place is for the exclusive use of yourself, family, and bona fide friends.
5. You may get a permit to move liquor when you change residences.
6. You may manufacture, sell, or transport liquor for non-beverage or sacramental purposes provided you obtain a government permit.
7. You cannot carry a hip flask.
8. You cannot give away or receive a bottle of liquor as a gift.
9. You cannot take liquor to hotels or restaurants and drink it in public dining rooms.
10. You cannot buy formulas or sell recipes for homemade liquors.
11. You cannot ship liquor for beverage use.
12. You cannot manufacture anything above one half of one percent (liquor strength) in your home. . . .

In 1919, Garrett had 17 grape pressing facilities across the country—in North Carolina, Virginia, New York, Ohio, Missouri and California. Production of wine in the U.S. that year was over 55 million gallons; the following year it dropped to 20 million gallons. In 1922, production was over 6 million gallons, and by 1925, it had dropped to 3,638,000 gallons.

When Prohibition loomed, Garrett was convinced that a national Prohibition would be short-lived. He was a strong believer that light wine was food, and that, eventually, the public would be allowed to buy it and drink it.

During Prohibition, Garrett produced a cola-grape drink called Satenet and flavoring extracts on which he lost money. He was slightly more successful with a mixture called Virginia Dare Tonic, which included beef extract and pepsin and could be sold legally. Although Garrett scaled down his facilities during Prohibition, his winery in Aberdeen, North Carolina, was the only one that he closed.

One seemingly contradictory activity occurred due to the provision in the Volstead Act permitting the legal production of "fruit juices" in the home. Section 29 of the Volstead Act allowed a homeowner to produce up to 200 gallons annually of "nonintoxicating cider and fruit juices exclusively for use in his home." Grape concentrate became increasingly popular with home winemakers. Each barrel of concentrate was shipped with a packet of yeast and a warning not to use it "because if you do, this will turn into wine, which would be illegal."

The price of grapes increased from $10 a ton to $100 a ton. In 1919, California had 300,000 acres of vineyards. By 1926, the acreage had doubled, and grape shipments increased by 125 percent. Unfortunately, oversupply destroyed the market, and by the end of Prohibition, grape growers were back where they started—pulling out their vines.

Garrett proposed to help the wine industry by selling grape concentrate in cans, complete with winemaking and bottling instructions, directly to the buyer's home. After an initial success, Garrett further proposed to aid the failing wine industry by letting the federal government's Farm Relief Program finance the effort.

In 1929, Garrett led a drive to form a combine called Fruit Industries, Inc., which included the largest wineries in California, the Vineyardists' Association, and the Garrett & Company wineries. Garrett had to relinquish the Virginia Dare label when he joined Fruit Industries. The combine hired Mabel Walker Willebrandt, who had been the assistant attorney general responsible for prosecuting violators of the Volstead Act, to ensure that it operated within Prohibition law. New York Governor Al Smith, leader of the Wets in U.S. politics, observed:

> I congratulate Fruit Industries in securing the services of so competent a person as Mabel. She did two things for them,

> two wonderful things. She convinced the Department of
> Justice that this 12 percent wine was not intoxicating.
> That was some stunt when you figure that old Andy
> Volstead fixed it at half of one percent, and she jumped it
> up 11 and a half percent and still robbed it of every intoxi-
> cating character. But she did something else for them that
> was equally important. She got the Farm Board to lend
> them $20,000,000.

Fruit Industries received substantial loans from the Federal Farm Board to "salvage the grape surplus" by converting it into grape concentrate called Vine-Glo. Nine varieties of Vine-Glo were offered: Port, Virginia Dare, Muscatel, Angelica, Tokay, Sauterne, Riesling, Claret, and Burgundy. Advertisements noted that wine made from Vine-Glo was legal according to Section 29 of the Volstead Act as long as it was not transported.

When the Drys saw the Vine-Glo ads, they reacted immediate-ly by bombarding Washington with protests. The Justice Department threatened to file a suit against Fruit Industries. The California Vineyardists' Association pleaded for the continuance of Vine-Glo without success. The product was removed from the market in 1931.

In the early 1930s, Garrett moved his headquarters to the Bush Terminal in Brooklyn, where Garrett & Company had substantial blending and bottling facilities.

Mission Vineyard and Winery, Cucamonga, California

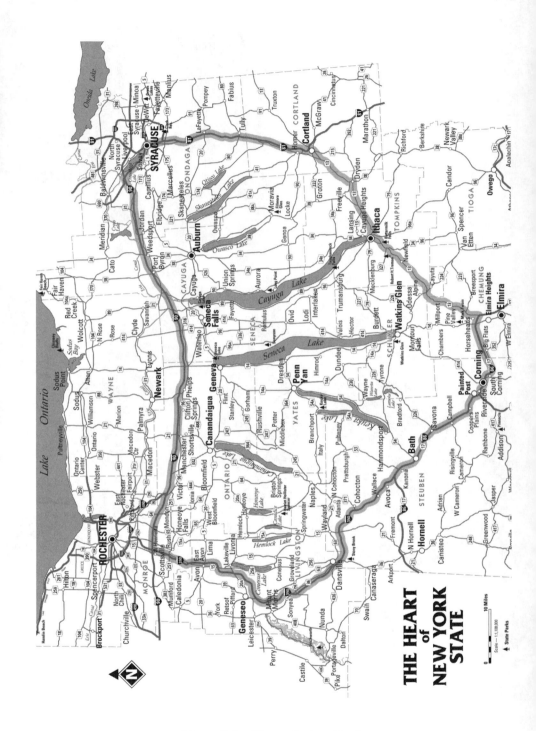

Map of the Finger Lakes Region

CHAPTER 8

The Wine Industry in the Finger Lakes Region

"The Finger Lakes—Canandaigua, Keuka, Seneca, Cayuga, Owasco, Skaneateles, and [five] others—are so long, narrow and parallel in their north-south direction that the Indians thought them the imprint of the hands of the Great Spirit. Scooped out by glacial action ages ago, these deep blue lakes make the [fourteen] counties of the district a spectacularly scenic vacation land. Among its chief attractions are the picturesque vineyards and wineries, most of which offer cellar tours and tasting hospitality to visitors.

"As in other vineyard regions that border bodies of water, the Finger Lakes temper the extremes of temperature along their shores and therefore protect the grapevines from the killing frosts of the spring and fall. The growing season here, though . . . shorter than California, is usually warm and dry to allow the grapes to ripen. In this respect, nearly every year in the Finger Lakes District is a vintage year—the envy of European winegrowers."

Leon Adams, *The Wines of America*

The wine region to which Paul Garrett moved when he left the South began in 1829 in the rectory garden of St. James Episcopal Church in Hammondsport, where Reverend William Bostwick introduced the first grapevines to the Finger Lakes Region. He planted Catawba and Isabella vines from the Hudson River Valley.

In 1848, Edward McKay planted 150 Isabella grapevines at Naples, at the southern end of Canandaigua Lake. The vines prospered, and an industry grew.

In 1853, Andrew Reisinger, a German vineyardist, planted two acres of Catawba and Isabella vines in Pulteney, north of Hammondsport, for which he used trellises; he became a pioneer in training grapevines. In *The Grapes of New York,* U. P. Hedrick observed of Reisinger: "Reisinger trained, pruned, and tilled his vines, operations unheard of before in the district, and was rewarded with crops and profits which stimulated grape culture in his and nearby neighborhoods."

The first bonded Finger Lakes Region winery was Pleasant Valley Winery, producer of Great Western Champagne, which began commercial production of wine in 1860 in Pleasant Valley, south of Hammondsport. Charles Champlin, the French winemaker who founded Pleasant Valley Winery, was granted U.S. Winery License No. 1. The Urbana Wine Company, renamed Gold Seal Winery in 1887, was founded in 1865. In 1880, Walter Taylor and his wife, Adie, founded Taylor Wine Company and began to produce wine.

John Jacob Widmer, founder of Widmer Wine Cellars, and his wife, Lisette, emigrated from Switzerland in 1882. They planted vineyards immediately upon their arrival in Naples and began making wine as soon as their vineyards matured. In 1910, the Widmers' son, Will, attended the Royal Wine School at Geisenheim, Germany. Widmer was one of the first wineries in the U.S. to offer "varietal" wines of one grape variety, as opposed to blended wines, and also was among the first to offer dated vintage wines.

When Garrett moved his headquarters to the Finger Lakes Region in 1912, he established vineyards and built a beautiful home on Keuka Lake's bluff, between the west and east branches of the Y-shaped lake. He also established wineries in Penn Yan and warehouses in Hammondsport at the southern end of Keuka Lake and in Canandaigua.

During Prohibition, 27 New York State wineries went out of business. Taylor and Widmer survived by making and selling grape juice and sacramental wine. The three sons of Walter and Adie Taylor, Greyton, Clarence, and Fred, purchased the Columbia Wine Company in Pleasant Valley and moved the Taylor operation to its stately headquarters building.

In 1934, president E. S. Underhill, Jr., of Gold Seal Winery, brought Charles Fournier, chief winemaker of Clicquot Ponsardin in Rheims, France, to Hammondsport as production manager to restore the winery's pre-Prohibition reputation. Fournier, educated at the University of Paris and at schools of enology in France and Switzerland, brought French-American hybrid grapes to area vineyards.

In 1943, Fournier successfully introduced his champagne, Charles Fournier Brut, to the U.S. market. In 1950, the California State Fair opened its wine competition to eastern and foreign wines. The only gold medal awarded was for Charles Fournier New York State Champagne.

Many changes occurred in the Finger Lakes wine region in the decades following Paul Garrett's death in 1940, including the introducing of Vinifera grape varieties in the 1950s and 1960s and the opening of boutique (farm) wineries beginning in the 1970s.

In 1953, Fournier hired Dr. Konstantin Frank to establish a *Vitis vinifera* grape nursery at Gold Seal. Dr. Frank had emigrated in 1951 from Ukraine, where he had been director of the Institute of Viticulture and Enology.

Dr. Frank convinced Fournier that past problems growing European varieties of grapes in the Finger Lakes Region were due to diseases, such as mildew, which could be controlled. Winter temperatures were not the principal problem. In addition, Dr. Frank suggested grafting *Vitis vinifera* vines onto hardy rootstock that would allow the canes of the vine to ripen before the first winter freeze.

In 1976, the New York State Legislature passed the Farm Winery Act. Removing the requirement for bonded wineries stimulated the Finger Lakes Region wine industry. Many vineyardists began to make wine instead of selling all of their grapes to wineries. By the early twenty-first century, over 100 wineries flourished in the Finger Lakes Region.

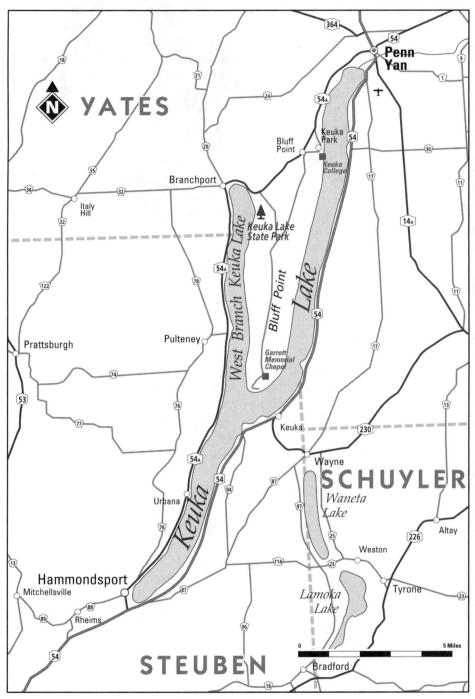

Map of Keuka Lake

CHAPTER 9

After the Repeal of Prohibition and Later Life

"Repeal, when it came in 1933, was met not so much with loud rejoicings as with a great public sigh of relief. Obviously the wine men had more reason than most to be joyful, but they had much to make them rueful too. The degenerate state of the vineyards . . . and of course the closing of the great majority of the wineries meant that the material basis of the industry had to be built all over again; buildings were out of repair or converted to other uses; machinery had been dispersed, or, if still in place, was out of order or obsolete; the vats and casks had been broken up or had dried out and fallen apart.

"More serious yet was the absence of experienced workers and managers: the continuity of tradition had been broken, and although there might be survivors who could pass on what they knew, there had been no young generation to receive it. That was the view on the production side. The market was equally derelict. The whole system of packaging, distributing, advertising, and selling wine had to be made anew."

Thomas Pinney, *A History of Wine in America from
the Beginnings to Prohibition*

The fourteen years of national Prohibition devastated the U.S. wine industry and had a lasting effect on its reputation. Many distinguished wineries had gone out of business, including Krug, "the wine king of the Napa Valley." Because California had more wineries than any other state, the impact of Prohibition, as elucidated by author Thomas Pinney, had been severe:

> There was no encouragement to plant the superior, more delicate, yet less attractive looking, varieties; indeed, there was every reason not to, when the market demanded the coarse, heavy bearing sorts. The result that the vast new plantings that went in during the Prohibition years were of the poorer sorts.

> The damage that this deterioration in the varietal quality of California's vineyards did to the reputation of California wines persisted long after Prohibition was a thing of the past. Table grapes, raisin grapes, and inferior, but productive, varieties of wine grapes were the overwhelming basis for California winemaking for years after Prohibition.

> Even as late as 1961, a whole generation after Repeal, there were only about 800 acres of Cabernet Sauvignon to supply the entire American wine industry! The same sorry figures held for the other distinguished varieties: 600 acres of Pinot Noir, 450 of Riesling, 300 of Chardonnay—absolutely appalling numbers when California already had 424,000 acres of vines.

New York State wineries survived Prohibition somewhat better than their California brethren. The Finger Lakes wineries, which were known for their highly regarded sparkling wines, had to rehire and add new workers to resume the production of champagne. Pleasant Valley Winery, known for its Great Western Champagne, survived and was later purchased by the Taylor Wine Company, which initially operated on a smaller scale than before Prohibition. Other Finger Lakes wineries that outlasted Prohibition were Gold Seal Winery in Hammondsport and Widmer Winery in Naples at the southern end of Canandaigua Lake.

With grape pressing facilities across the country—in North Carolina, Virginia, New York, Ohio, Missouri and California, when Prohibition was repealed in 1933, Garrett was the only vintner who could supply wine to all Wet States. Returning to the wine business after Repeal was complicated by the confusion that existed in local legislation. Garrett traveled throughout the South, advocating planting additional Scuppernong vineyards.

One of the pro-wine members of the federal government at the time of Repeal was Rexford Guy Tugwell, assistant secretary of the Department of Agriculture, an early member of FDR's "brain trust." He viewed wine as the drink of moderation and civility. Like Garrett, Tugwell considered wine as food, an agricultural product that should be widely available and inexpensive.

In *The Battle for Democracy,* Tugwell reasoned: "I foresee that, with this change in the drinking habits of our people, may come a change of temper and of temperament, a less furious striving for happiness at the bottom of the whiskey barrel.

"I foresee fewer deaths from heart failure, fewer nervous breakdowns, far fewer of the myriad ailments brought about by overwork and overworry. In their place, I anticipate a calmer and more leisurely type of civilization, in which there will be time for friendly conversation, philosophical speculation, gaiety, and substantial happiness."

Tugwell authorized a plan for a program of research in viticulture and enology. The plan noted that "winemaking in the United States has remained up to the present in the group of arts and crafts and has never become a science . . . If the resumption of wine manufacture in the United States is to result in anything other than a repetition of past history, with a resultant flooding of our markets with an inferior product which is discriminated against by purchasers in favor of foreign wines, the initiation of a strong program of research for the guidance of the industry into scientific methods of production is absolutely necessary."

The plan included the construction of a model winery at the Beltsville, Maryland, agriculture station, which would be the headquarters for research. Model wineries in other parts of the country were included in the plan, including one in California, which would be run in cooperation with the University of California.

In 1933, when Garrett severed connections with the extensive marketing cooperative Fruit Industries, he recovered his right to the Virginia Dare trade name, which he had to surrender when he joined the combine. Unfortunately, in exchange, he had to forfeit his California wine reserves worth millions of dollars.

Beginning in 1934, Garrett attempted to convince California winegrowers of the advantage of blending native *Vitis labrusca* grape varieties (high acid, low sugar) from the East, such as Concord, Delaware, and Ives, with European *Vitis vinifera* grape varieties (low acid, high sugar) from the West. He was ahead of his time with this proposal. By 1970, the large California wineries began to blend *Vitis labrusca* concentrates and juice from other states with their juice.

New York State grape growers did not have an organization like California's Wine Institute to address their needs and to communicate their interests. Garrett became their spokesman. *Fortune* magazine called him the "Dean of American Winemen" in its February 1934 issue. The November 4, 1935, New York *Times* referred to him as "Dean of American Wine Growers."

With experience in the wine industry dating back to 1877 and with knowledge in vine management, winemaking, marketing, and distribution, Garrett was the logical person to become a spokesperson for vineyardists and winemakers. His location in New York City, the financial and communications center of the U.S., encouraged his choice. Garrett's opinions on the wine industry were expressed in interviews, letters to the New York *Times*, and three pamphlets published in 1934 and 1935. He was the foremost promoter of American wine for Americans. In an article in the November 4, 1935, New York *Times*, he advocated viewing table wine as food, which would encourage increased production of table wine and assist in developing the wine industry in the U.S.

In 1905, Garrett had written *The Art of Serving Wine,* hoping that disseminating information about wine would help to increase its market. Also, he later contracted for the first singing commercial on radio for an alcoholic beverage: "Say it again, Virginia Dare, it's such a delicious wine."

Garrett recommended legislation that would remove table wine from the liquor category, thus freeing it from the regulations and taxes associated with the manufacture and sale of distilled spirits:

"Legislation classifying table wine as food, in conjunction with a sufficiently high tariff, would result in the planting of five million acres of American land to produce two and one-half billion gallons of wine, and the pleasant and profitable employment of 17 million people in viticulture." Garrett further expanded this theme in the October 1939 issue of *Wines and Vines*:

> One of the biggest drawbacks to America's wine industry today is that wine is too high priced. In Europe, where wine is cheap, rich and poor alike drink it. There is a major industry in countries such as France, Spain, Portugal, Greece, and Germany, giving employment directly or indirectly to a large element of the population. I believe that if the government would reduce the high taxes on wine by 50 percent, America's consumption of wine would rapidly increase to such an extent that America would soon have a new major industry to supply the demand for wine.

Paul Garrett died on March 18, 1940, in Roosevelt Hospital in New York after contracting pneumonia following surgery. He had been in New York promoting American wines. He was survived by his widow, Evelyn Edwards Garrett and three daughters: Dorothy, Evelyn, and Emily. Funeral services were held in the Garrett Memorial Chapel on Bluff Point, Keuka Lake, that the Garretts had built in memory of their son, Charles, who died at the age of 26. The Bishop of the Episcopal Diocese of Rochester officiated. Garrett was laid to rest in a vault alongside his three sons who had died in infancy and his son, Charles.

Apparently Garrett's gamble to give up his California wine inventory to regain the Virginia Dare trade name had paid off by the time of his death in 1940, and his heirs were able to expand to meet the demand for Garrett & Company wine. In 1943, they purchased a substantial vineyard and winery in Ukiah, California, and in 1945 gained control of the huge holdings of the Italian Vineyard Company at Guasti. With these two properties added to the existing property at Cucamonga, Garrett & Company owned 7,000 acres of vineyards and three of the largest grape processing plants on the West Coast. All bottling was done at Guasti or at the Bush Terminal bottling facility in Brooklyn.

Paul Garrett

When the value of Los Angeles real estate skyrocketed, Garrett & Company began to sell some of its property in the region. In 1961, Garrett & Company liquidated its business to take advantage of the increased value of its assets. Alta Vineyards of Fresno obtained the rights to the Garrett labels. When Alta Vineyards merged with the Guild Federation in Lodi, California, the Virginia Dare trade name went with the merger. In 1966, the Canandaigua Wine Company of the Finger Lakes Region obtained the use of the trade name. The Virginia Dare trade name lived on long after the death of its creator.

Garrett Home, Keuka Lake

WILL

There is no chance, no destiny, no fate,

Can circumvent or hinder or control

The firm resolve of a determined soul.

Gifts count for nothing; will alone is great;

All things give way before it, sooner or later.

What obstacle can stay the mighty force

Of the sea-seeking river in its course,

Or cause the ascending orb of day to wait?

Each wellborn soul must win what it deserves.

Let the fool prate of luck. The fortunate

Is he whose earnest purpose never swerves,

Whose slightest action or inaction serves

The one great aim. Why, even Death stands still,

And waits an hour sometimes for such a will.

Ella Wheeler Wilcox

EPILOGUE

What We Can Learn from Paul Garrett's Life

"It is when things go hardest, when life becomes most trying that there is the greatest need for a fixed goal, for having an air castle that the outside world cannot wreck. When few comforts come from without, it is all the more necessary to have a fount to draw from within, and the man or woman who has a star toward which to press cannot be thrown off the course, no matter how the world may try, no matter how far things may seem to be wrong."

Walter S. Taylor, founder of Bully Hill Vineyards, Hammondsport, New York

Garrett realized that the chances of success are increased substantially if also we are doing what we want to do and what we are good at doing. Author Mark Sullivan observed:

> To find a career to which you are adapted by nature and then to work hard at it is about as near a formula for success and happiness as the world provides. One of the fortunate aspects of this formula is that, granted that the right career has been found, the hard work takes care of itself. Then hard work is not hard at all.

During his lifetime, Garrett displayed the qualities of determination and perseverance on many occasions. A Mark Twain perception could have been written about Garrett: "The miracle, the power, that elevates the few is to be found in their industry, application, and perseverance under the promptings of a determined spirit."

As noted in the chapter on overcoming obstacles, Garrett was also known for the personal characteristic of resilience. Author Leon Adams met "the fabulous Captain Paul Garrett" in the early 1930s and described him as a tall, portly, forceful man with a deep voice and a soft southern accent. The key word is "forceful."

After the Panic of 1893 and despite bankers' fears about the potential negative economic impact of the outcome of the 1896 Presidential election, Garrett gambled on expansion with loans from Richmond banks, including the building of a new warehouse that soon required additions. He commented on his "first real necessity of enlarged operations by accumulating larger inventories of goods, always one of my hobbies—which has stood me in good stead." Author Clarence Gohdes noted:

> When what he called his "expanding spree" dominated his decisions, his gambles were matched only by the renewed efforts he put forth. . . . There is of course no single clue to a man's character, but something of Garrett's amazing drive may be glimpsed in his phrases like "one of my hobbies" or "my expanding sprees." Business was a game to be played, the risks many, the rewards, ultimately in millions, a secondary result of riding a hobby, or perhaps appropriately for a vintner, going on a "spree."

The Roanoke *News* noted about Garrett & Company that "the winery was not only one of the largest in the region, its wares sold from Maine to California, but its owner was a 'level-headed businessman with push and energy in him of any ten men.'" These observations illustrate two of Garrett's strong personal qualities: his willingness to take risks and his drive.

Garrett recognized the importance of setting goals. He knew that a goal might be aggressive, but it should be attainable. He moved on from one accomplished goal to another.

While still a young man, shortly after the death of his father and his young wife, Garrett seriously considered going to South Africa and joining Cecil Rhodes in managing diamond and gold mines. He told no one of these plans, and he might have gone if the relatives to whom he had temporarily turned over the running of Garrett & Company had not lost the accumulated capital that he had earned. He was a broad enough thinker to consider a completely different career on another continent.

Garrett stayed in the wine business and with his combination of strong personal characteristics was immensely successful. Paul Garrett's life is worthy of emulation. We can learn from him.

Paul Garrett

The Chapel on the Mount, Bluff Point, Keuka Lake

APPENDIX

The Chapel on the Mount

"At the last interview with his mother, just before his death when they talked of going 'back home,' [Garrett's son] Charles's eyes filled with tears when she was leaving, as he remarked, 'Don't leave me out here [Tucson, Arizona]. Take me home to Bluff Point, take me home.'

"[That] gave birth to the idea [of building a chapel]. And this idea is not that merely of a place of sepulcher, but rather a shrine from which may radiate the fine ideals of young manhood, so that while deprived of doing the work that an ambitious young man dreams of, those virtues which he manifested in all his human relations with young and old, may radiate, and with the coming years and centuries grow with increasing lustre as time adds legend and poetry and idealisms to the memory of the family, united in death as in life."

Paul Garrett

Garrett Memorial Chapel, constructed in the style of sixth-century Saxon architecture, was built in 1931 by Paul and Evelyn Edwards Garrett in memory of their son, Charles Williams Garrett, who died at the age of 26 of tuberculosis. Charles attended preparatory school at Culver Military Academy and at Phillips Exeter Academy in Andover, Massachusetts, and graduated with honors from Yale University in 1927.

The chapel, referred to by Paul Garrett as the "Little Chapel on the Mount," is located near the tip of Bluff Point. The Garretts owned 50 acres of land on the Bluff, including 1,000 feet of lake frontage. The chapel and the land on which it was built were deeded to the Episcopal Diocese of Rochester. The chapel is maintained by an endowment fund and is open to the public at scheduled times, including Sundays in July and August for worship services. It is the burial site for the Garrett family.

The chapel was designed by Mortimer Freehof, who chose materials from around the world. The floor of the chapel is constructed of Rembrandt slate from Holland, the walls are of seamface granite from Pennsylvania, and the floor of the terrace and the roof are of Vermont slate. The reception room walls are craborchard marble from Tennessee, and the marble in the crypt is onyx from Algeria. The steel trusses supporting the roof have the appearance of oak beams. In planning the windows, Garrett's intent was to emphasize the commandment "love thy neighbor as thyself" and to convey the message that a civilization that endures can only be built on a foundation of the family with love at the center of family life. The chapel's interior reveals considerable symbolism. As described by Paul Garrett:

> The carved stone statue above the chapel entrance symbolizes youth looking quizzically on the world, which he holds in his hands as though to see how he could shape it better; mould it to higher standards of ethical conduct and right living.
>
> The stone cherub at the corner of the tower symbolizes eternal life—rebirth in the spirit of immortal childhood.
>
> The decorations of the vine, the grape, the oak leaf, the acorn, the primrose and other symbols of life and growth are shown in stone and plaster.
>
> The ship weather vane is the symbol of enterprise and the discoverer seeking new worlds to discover.
>
> The lovebirds, guarding the nest of the young, are symbolic of family devotion and life.
>
> The bronze door to the crypt lobby shows pictorially the phases of human activities, art and architecture, music and painting, science and astronomy.
>
> All are crowned by motherhood, that finest expression of love.

In designing the stained glass windows, Frederick Wilson departed from stereotyped ecclesiastical designs. His intent was for the first window to illustrate a picture of immortality in nature represented by Alfred, Lord Tennyson's *The Brook*: "And men may come and men may go, but I go on forever." The second window is of Sir Galahad, "whose strength is the strength of ten," seeking the Holy Grail. The border displays events in the progress of civilization, such as the Star of Bethlehem, the Norman conquest, the Bill of Rights, the Magna Carta, the printing press, the liberty bell, and a Curtiss airplane developed in Hammondsport. The third window illustrates the three small children from Eugene Field's poem *Wynken, Blynken, and Nod* sailing into their dreams in an old shoe rigged with a sail to go "fishing for the stars."

The theme of the poem, *Abou Ben Adhem*, by James Henry Leigh Hunt, is displayed in the fourth window with the request to the angel writing in the Book of Gold: "I pray thee, then, write me as one that loves his fellow men." The angel "showed the names whom love of God had blessed. And, lo! Ben Adhem's name led all the rest!" The fifth window depicts "Mother Love" with a look of defiance as she defends her child from attack by a vulture (sin). In the margin of this window is a pelican, the bird that feeds its young with drops of blood squeezed from its own breast, as a symbol of the self-sacrificing love of Christ.

The theme of the next window is Henry Wadsworth Longfellow's *Children's Hour*, with children coming downstairs in the hour before bedtime and attempting to delay bedtime by playing with their parents, who are saying "time to be in bed." The children's blocks contain the phrases: "Carry on," "Peace with honor," and "God is love, love is God." The border of the window is comprised of characters from Mother Goose nursery rhymes, such as "Little Bo Peep" and "The Cow Jumped Over the Moon."

The window in the west end depicts Tennyson's *Crossing the Bar*. In this window the soul is shown majestically with a full sail, a fresh wind, and angels transporting it to the great beyond with the words: "Sunset and evening star, and one clear call for me. . . . And may there be no mourning at the bar, when I put to sea."

Paul Garrett

PRESS ON

Nothing in the world can take the place of persistence.

Talent will not; nothing is more common than unsuccessful men with talent.

Genius will not; unrewarded genius is almost a proverb.

Education will not; the world is full of educated derelicts.

Persistence and determination alone are omnipotent.

Anonymous

(Appeared on the cover of a program for a memorial service for Calvin Coolidge in 1933.)

BIBLIOGRAPHY

Adams, Leon. *The Wines of America.* Boston: Houghton Mifflin, 1973.

Allen, H. Warner. *A History of Wine.* London: Faber and Faber, 1961.

Behr, Edward. *Prohibition: Thirteen Years That Changed America.* New York: Arcade Publishing, 1996.

Cool, R. C. *The Scuppernong Grape: Its Growth and Care Under Vineyard Conditions.* Raleigh: Edwards & Broughton, 1913.

Cotten, Sallie Southall. *The White Doe: The Fate of Virginia Dare.* Philadelphia: J. B. Lippincott, 2001.

Garrett, Paul. *Reminiscences.* Self-published, 1940.

—. "Classing of Wine As Food Is Urged." New York *Times,* November 4, 1935.

—. "Virtue in Wines." New York *Times,* December 8, 1935.

Gohdes, Clarence. *Scuppernong: North Carolina's Grape and Its Wines.* Durham: Duke University Press, 1982.

Hedrick, U. P. *The Grapes of New York.* Albany: State of New York, 1908.

Jackisch, Philip. *Modern Winemaking.* Ithaca: Cornell University Press, 1985.

Johnson, Hugh. *Pocket Encyclopedia of Wine.* New York: Simon & Schuster, 1998.

Klees, Emerson. *Persons, Places, and Things Of the Finger Lakes Region.* Rochester, New York: Friends of the Finger Lakes Publishing, 2009.

—. *Wineries of the Finger Lakes Region.* Rochester, New York: Friends of the Finger Lakes Publishing, 2008.

Lichine, Alexis, et. al., *New Encyclopedia of Wine and Spirits.* New York: Alfred A. Knopf, 1974.

Morton, Lucie T. *Winegrowing in Eastern America: An Illustrated Guide to Viticulture East of the Rockies.* New York: Alfred A. Knopf, 1985.

New York *Times.* "Paul Garrett Dies: Noted Wine Maker." March 20, 1940.

Pinney, Thomas. *A History of Wine in America from the Beginnings to Prohibition*, vol. 1. Berkeley: University of California Press, 1989.

Paul Garrett

—. *A History of Wine in America from Prohibition to the Present*, vol. 2. Berkeley: University of California Press, 2005.

Robinson, Jancis. *Guide to Wine Grapes*. New York: Oxford University Press, 1996.

Schoonmaker, Frank. *The Encyclopedia of Wine*. New York: Hastings House, 1973.

Tugwell, Rexford Guy. *The Battle for Democracy*. New York: Columbia University Press, 1935.

Van Buren, J. *The Scuppernong Grape, Its History and Mode of Cultivation: With a Short Treatise on the Manufacture of Wine From It*. Memphis: Goodwyn & Co., 1872.

Wagner, Philip M. *Grapes Into Wine: The Art of Winemaking in America*. New York: Alfred A. Knopf, 1976.

—. *A Wine-grower's Guide*. New York: Alfred A. Knopf, 1973.

Wayward Tendrils Newsletter. Vol. 9, No. 4, October 1999, pp 2, 3.

Winkler, A. J. *General Viticulture*. Berkeley: University of California Press, 1962.

INDEX

11-12
14.95

T 569595

DUE	